The Event

songbook

music edition

KINGSWAY MUSIC

EASTBOURNE

United Kingdom: CCL (Europe), PO Box 1339, Eastbourne, East Sussex, BN21 1AD

United States: CCLI, 17201 NE Sacramento Street, Portland, Oregon 97230, USA

Australasia: CCL Asia Pacific Pty Ltd, PO Box 6644, Baulkham Hills Business Centre,
NSW 2153, Australia

Africa: CCL Africa Ltd, PO Box 2347, Durbanville 7551, South Africa

ISBN 1 84291 025 6

Biblical quotations are taken from the New International Version,
(c) 1973, 1978, 1984 by the International Bible Society.
Published by Hodder & Stoughton and used by permission.

Music setting by David Ball.

Music arrangers: David Ball, Chris Norton, Michael Sandeman, Stuart Townend.

Cover design by Julia Evetts.
Original Cover Photo by Mark Evetts.

Printed in the United Kingdom by Halstan & Co. Ltd., Amersham, Bucks for
KINGSWAY COMMUNICATIONS LTD
Lottbridge Drove, Eastbourne, East Sussex, BN23 6NT, UK.

Index of Titles and First Lines

The songs appear in alphabetical order by first line, not necessarily by author's title, for easy use in praise and worship meetings. To further faciliate the use of this book, where possible all two-page piano arrangements appear on facing pages to avoid turning over, while maintaining the alphabetical order. Authors' titles, where different from first lines, are shown in *italics*.

1.

A humble heart
(Won't let go)

Brian Houston

Country rock feel

1. A hum-ble heart You have yet to de-spise,

and so I hum-ble my-self in this place.

If they that sow in tears shall reap in joy,

let a mil-lion tears or more roll down my face.

If You don't an-swer me to-day, Lord,

Event 01/02

won't let go ___ till You bless ___ me, ___ Lord. ___ And I will cry ___ out to You ___ till I can't ___ cry no more. And I ___ won't let go ___ till You bless ___ me ___ Lord. ___ ___ me ___ Lord. ___

2. Where can I go if You don't bid me go?
   And I have no hope if You are not my hope.
   And I have no peace if You don't give me peace,
   And I have no faith if You don't help me to believe.
   If You don't answer me today
   Will the heathen nations mock Your name
   And say You're made of wood or clay?
   Ah, but I've seen You provide for me,
   I've kissed Your lips and felt You heal my pain.
   Hey, can You do it once again?

   'Cause I won't let go till You bless me, Lord...

2.   All of me

Gareth Robinson

Worshipfully

All of me,___ all of me___ I give___ to___ You,___
more of You___ I long___ for,

— on-ly You,___ Je - sus.___

More of You,___ For this life___ I live for You.

I tru - ly wor-ship You,___ All of my___ days,___

in ev - 'ry way.___ I will praise You

3.

Almighty God

Mark Vargeson

4.

And after all

(Unashamed)

Capo 3(G)

With energy

Paul Oakley

1.) And af-ter all,___ ev-'ry-thing___
To lose it all,___ and find a Friend___

___ I___ once held dear just proved___ to be___ so
___ who's___ al-ways near could on - ly be___ my

___ vain. And when I think___ of what___ You've done___
___ gain.

___ for me,___ to bring me to___ the Fa-ther's

___ side:___ Un-a-shamed___ and un - a-fraid,___
Un-a-shamed___ and un - a-fraid,___

Mid section

(I'm un - a -

I know some___ will say___ it's fool-ish-ness:

You can't make___ a blind - man___ see.

But I know___ that there___ is pow - er in the cross

to save___ those___ who be - lieve.___

Fine

D.S.

2. Could it be
   That You should put on human flesh,
   Your glory laid aside?
   Bruised for me,
   Majesty upon the cross,
   Forsaken and despised.
   When I think of what it cost for You,
   To bring me to the Father's side:

The Lord will be king over the whole earth. On that day there will be one Lord, and His name the only name.

ZECHARIAH 14:9

5. And I'm forgiven

(You are my King)

Billy James Foote

Worshipfully

Verse

And I'm for-gi-ven,— be-cause You were— for-sa-ken.

And I'm ac-cep-ted:— You were— con-demned.—

And I'm a-live— and well,— Your Spi-rit is— with-in— me,— be-

cause You died— and rose— a-gain.— A-ma-zing love,— how—

_can it be— that You, my King,— would die— for me?—

Chorus

Event 01/02

6. Beauty for ashes

Capo 3(D)

Neil Bennetts

Steadily

Beau-ty for ash - es and gar-ments of praise,—— You come and a-dorn—— me with joy once a-gain—— and pour oil of glad - ness in - stead of de-spair,—— bring-ing Your mer - cy a-gain,—— like sweet spring rain.—— Sweet spring rain,—— mer-cy from hea - ven, sweet spring rain,—

Event 01/02

7.

Breathe on me

Capo 1(D)

Andrea Lawrence
& Noel Robinson

With intensity

Breathe on me, ___ O wind of change, ___ a-
noint me with ___ fresh oil ___ from Your throne. ___ Lord, re-store
___ me with ___ new ___ life, ___ so I'm rea - dy to serve ___ and I'm ready to go, ___ rea - dy to do ___ Your will. ___ So I'm ready to serve ___ and I'm rea - dy to go, ___ rea - dy to do ___ Your will.

Event 01/02

Lord, help me to run this race— and to live— by Your grace,

— all I want to do—— is Your will.——

Rea-dy to serve,— rea-dy to go,— rea-dy to do,— rea-dy to be,—

rea - dy to do—— Your will.——

8.
Come, let us worship

Nathan Fellingham

Event 01/02

9.
Give thanks to the Lord
(Forever)

Moderato

Chris Tomlin

2. With a mighty hand and an outstretched arm,
   His love endures forever.
   For the life that's been reborn.
   His love endures forever.
   Sing praise, sing praise,
   Sing praise, sing praise.

3. From the rising to the setting sun,
   His love endures forever.
   By the grace of God, we will carry on.
   His love endures forever.
   Sing praise, sing praise,
   Sing praise, sing praise.

10.

God is our Father

(Kingdom of heaven our goal)

David Lyle Morris
& Nick Wynne-Jones

Gently

1. God is our Father in heaven above, and He cares for His children with infinite love. Our worries are needless, look up in the sky where carefree and singing the birds freely fly. Their Maker who knows them, supplies all their food, how much more is our

Fa - ther con - cerned for our good?

Chorus
For our Fa - ther in hea - ven knows all of our needs, He will

care for us al - ways, we sur - ren - der our all, and make the

king - dom of hea - ven our goal.

2. Look at the lilies
   And see how they grow:
   They are clothed by God's goodness
   In beautiful show.
   Our Father in heaven
   Who cares for each flower,
   Provides for us always
   So great is His power.

   (Bridge 2.)
   The kingdom of heaven
   And His righteousness
   We will seek with a passion
   So all may be blessed.

11.

Good and gracious

Gareth Robinson

Good_____ and gra - cious,_____ att - ri - butes___ of a lo - ving Fath - er, You're high_____ and migh - ty,___ but hum - ble all the same._____ You have made the hea - vens and___ the earth,___ and You made us___ in Your im - age, Lord._____ Ho - ly, ho - ly, ho - ly is___ the___ Lord Al - migh - ty, and

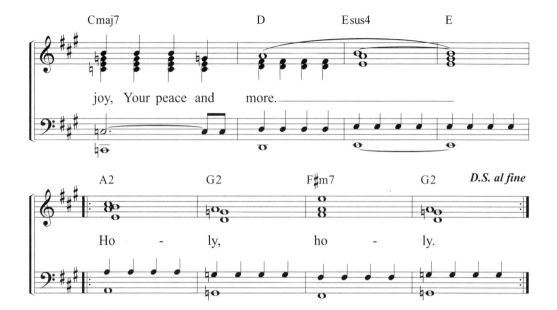

joy, Your peace and more.

Ho - ly, ho - ly.

2. Death and hell are now no longer things I fear because
   You have saved me and I'm grateful to the core.
   I'm Your child because of Jesus' blood,
   And Your Spirit leads me, guides me, fills me.

To Him who is able to keep you from falling and to present you before His glorious presence without fault and with great joy – to the only God our Saviour be glory, majesty, power and authority, through Jesus Christ our Lord, before all ages, now and for evermore! Amen.

JUDE: 24-25

12.

Heaven opened

(Praise)

Ken Riley

With energy

1. Heav - en o - pened_ and_ You came_____ to save me._ You were bro - ken_ and_ be - came_ sin for_ me.

2. You have ri - sen_ from_ the grave_____ for-ever,_ through e - ter - ni - ty_ I'll praise_ my Sa - viour.

No death, no hate, no shame, no slave a - gain_ to fear;_____ new life, new

Event 01/02

13. Hey Lord, O Lord

Event 01/02

14.

Holy, holy

Robin Mark

Simply

1. Ho-ly, ho-ly, ho-ly, ho-ly is the Lord God Al-migh-ty. Ho-ly, ho-ly, ho-ly, ho-ly is the song a-round the throne. Where the an-gels and the el-ders ga-ther there in sweet as-sem-bly, sing-ing ho-ly, sing-ing ho-ly is the Lord our God. 2. Wor-thy, wor-

2. *Chorus*

The Way, the Truth,— the Life,— the Light,—

— the King,— the Great— I— AM.—

My life,— my all,— my e - v'ry breath,—

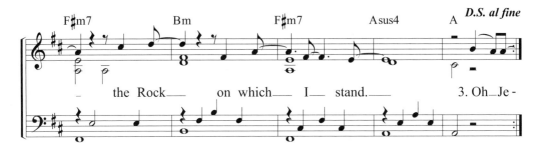

D.S. al fine

— the Rock— on which— I— stand.— 3. Oh— Je -

2. Worthy, worthy, worthy, worthy
   Is the Lamb who was slain for me.
   Worthy, worthy, worthy, worthy
   Is the song within my heart.
   I could choose to spend eternity
   With this sole refrain:
   Singing worthy, singing worthy
   Is the Lord our God.

3. Oh Jesus, oh Jesus,
   How You suffered and died for us.
   Oh Jesus, oh Jesus,
   But that tomb is empty now.
   And I long to gaze upon Your throne
   And all Your risen glory:
   Singing Jesus, singing Jesus
   Is the Lord of all.

15. Hope has found its home within me
(For this cause)

Joel Houston

Steadily

1. Hope has found its home with-in me

now that I've been found in You.

Let all I am be all You want me to be,

'cause all I want is more of You,

all I want is more of You.

2. Let Your presence fall upon us,
   I want to see You face to face;
   Let me live forever lost in Your love,
   'Cause all I want is more of You,
   All I want is more of You.

16.
I am helplessly in love with You
(I can only give my heart)

Worshipfully

Sue Rinaldi, Caroline Bonnett
& Steve Bassett

1. I am helplessly in love with You. I am lost in something precious. I am drowning in the sea of You. I am found amongst Your treasures. And I don't know why You give Yourself, And I can't explain why

Event 01/02

It's like brea-thing strange new— air,— walk-ing on some

dis-tant moon.——— I'll sing a song from the

depths of my soul:— seek-ing, find-ing, com-ing home.—

Seek-ing, find-ing, com-ing home.———

2. I am helplessly devoted to You;
   I am scorched by strange new fire.
   I am running deeper into You.
   I am high upon the wire.

17.
I am so tired of compromising
(Set me on fire)

Ryan Delmore

place Your love in - side.____

I want to go____ a-gainst____ the____ grain,____

I want to go____ a-gainst____ the____ grain.____

D.S. al Coda

Coda

18.
I come to You
(Your love)

Louise & Nathan Fellingham

Tenderly

1. I come to You,— to sit at Your feet,— I hear You call,— I'm long-ing to meet— You. I lift my face— to You, and catch Your eye,— oh how You sa-tis-fy.— Je-sus, Your love— sur-rounds me.— Je-sus, Your love— com-

2. Now looking closer, I see the scars,
   Stories of love,
   You paid the greatest price,
   So that I may have life.
   Thank You, my Friend,
   You're showing me once again.

19. I count as nothing every earthly treasure

Neil Bennetts

I count as no-thing ev-'ry earth-ly trea-sure, Je-sus;
Why would I look for a-ny world-ly plea-sure, Je-sus,

what You have shown me is that You are the source of my life.
when I have all things in You? And just a heart-beat a-way.

So what else can I do but stay
So what else can I do but stay

here?
here with You?

You're all that I need, You're all that I need,

Event 01/02

so here I'll stay_____ and give my praise_____

to You._____

20.

I have come to realise

Andrew Rogers

Rhythmically

I have come to re - a-lise— the glo-ry of the Lord— re-sides—

in this jar— of— clay. And

if my world is going to see— the glo-ry of the Lord— re-vealed,—

then my— pride— must— break. Then the fra-grance of

Je - sus will be re - leased,—

A   E/G♯   F♯m

I will live___ all my days___ to be the praise_____

B   E   ***D.S. al Coda***

_   of Your glo - ry.

Coda ⊕

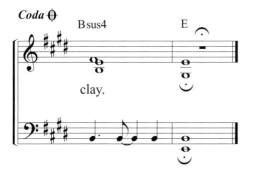

B sus4   E

clay.

21.

I look into the eyes of love

Doug Hawkins

Lyrics:

1. I look in-to the eyes__ of__ love,__ and I see joy un-end-ing;__ my Fa-ther's face shines__ on me.__ _____ Your waves of grace come crash-ing__ in,__ re-mov-ing ev-'ry blot__ of__ sin,__

close when I cry.———— Ne-ver leav-ing,

e-ver pre-sent, al-ways by my side;——— You are— my

2nd time D.S.

heart's true— de-sire.——————

2. And now I stand before the throne,
For I've been counted righteous,
Because of blood shed for me.
Here I will join the massive throng,
As we all sing salvation's song,
The Son of God has set us free!

22. I love You more each day

Gently

Ken Riley

love___ You more each day,___ with all my__ heart can___

give;___ wor - ship at Your feet,___

lost with - in Your gaze.___ Just to__ know that You're near, my

Event 01/02

23.

In Christ alone

Capo 1 (D)

Words: Stuart Townend
Music: Keith Getty

Steadily

1. In Christ a - lone my hope is found, He is my light, my strength, my song; this Cor - ner - stone, this so - lid Ground, firm through the fier - cest drought and storm. What heights of love, what depths of peace, when fears are stilled, when striv - ings cease! My Com - for - ter, my All in

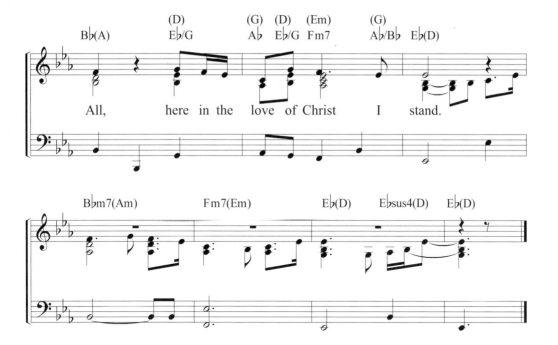

All, here in the love of Christ I stand.

2. In Christ alone! - who took on flesh,
   Fulness of God in helpless babe!
   This gift of love and righteousness,
   Scorned by the ones He came to save:
   Till on that cross as Jesus died,
   The wrath of God was satisfied -
   For every sin on Him was laid;
   Here in the death of Christ I live.

3. There in the ground His body lay,
   Light of the world by darkness slain:
   Then bursting forth in glorious Day
   Up from the grave He rose again!
   And as He stands in victory
   Sin's curse has lost its grip on me,
   For I am His and He is mine -
   Bought with the precious blood of Christ.

4. No guilt in life, no fear in death,
   This is the power of Christ in me;
   From life's first first cry to final breath,
   Jesus commands my destiny.
   No power of hell, no scheme of man,
   Can ever pluck me from His hand;
   Till He returns or calls me home,
   Here in the power of Christ I'll stand!

24.

In awe of You
(You are near)

Reuben Morgan

Flowing

In awe of You, we wor - ship,

and stand a - mazed at Your great love.

We're changed from glo -

ry to glo - ry, we set our hearts

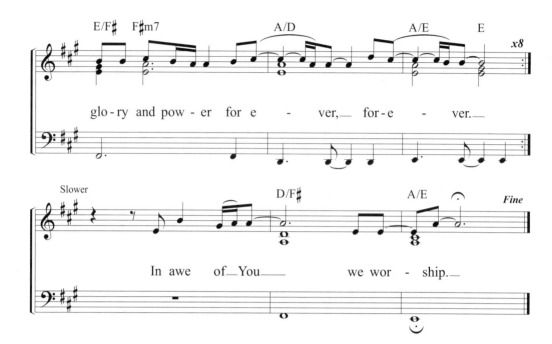

glo - ry and pow - er for e - ver,— for - e - ver.—

In awe of—You___ we wor - ship.—

25.

In every day that dawns

(I know You love me)

Kate Simmonds
& Stuart Townend

With a steady rhythm

1. In ev-'ry day that dawns, I see the light of Your splen-dour a-round— me; and ev-'ry-where I turn, I know the gift of Your fa - vour up-on— me. What can I do— but give— You glo-ry, Lord? Ev - 'ry-thing good— has come— from You.—

2. Through all that I have known,
   I have been held in the shelter of Your hand;
   And as my life unfolds,
   You are revealing the wisdom of Your sovereign plan.
   There are no shadows in Your faithfulness,
   There are no limits to Your love.

26.

In this place we gather

Stuart Plumb

In this place— we ga - ther to wor-ship You—
_ to - ge - ther, to come be - fore— You, ho - ly God.
And as we seek— Your face,
let this be Your dwell - ing place,— we have come—
_ to wor - ship You.— We come to give—

27. I see You hanging there
(For the cross)

Capo 3(D)

Michael Sandeman

With intensity

1. I see You hang-ing there,— nailed to a splin-tered wood-en beam,— drink-ing pain and sor - rows, breath - ing a - go - ny.— And I

And in those dark, dark hours,— as life drained from Your flesh and bones,— I know my life had its— be - gin - ning at— Your cross.—

thank— You, thank— You: For the cross,— where You bled, for the cross,— where You died,— for the cross,—

Event 01/02

2. You were my substitute
   In laying down Your life for mine,
   Being cursed and bearing
   The wrath of God for me.
   You were crushed by sin,
   Your punishment has brought me peace,
   And by the wounds You suffered
   I'm alive and healed.
   And I thank You, thank You:

3. Two days in the grave,
   Then You rose up from the dead -
   Now You reign in glory,
   Rule in righteousness.
   And I was raised with You,
   Free at last from all my sin,
   Safe forever in the shelter of my King.
   And I thank You, thank You:

28.

I've filled my days with details
(Be still)

David Gate

1. I've filled my days with de-tails___ and all the choi-ces of___ the earth,___ car-ried the yoke of wor-ry,___ and all the burd-ens that___ it brings.___ And through the midst of all___ the rush-ing, You___ whis-per to___ our hearts,___ and with___ Your

Event 01/02

2. So give me peace and wisdom
   To know how to fill my time,
   Where I can learn to keep You
   At the centre of my life.
   So through the midst of all the rushing
   There is time to spend with You,
   And my foundation will daily be:

*Find rest, O my soul, in God
alone; my hope comes from Him.
My salvation and my honour depend
on God; He is my mighty rock, my
refuge.*

PSALM 62:5, 7

29.
I will come

Capo 1 (D)

(All)

Tim Sherrington

Rhythmically, with anticipation
Verse

Cm(Bm)   Ab(G)   Eb(D)

1. I will come,— come, come— to the wa-ters— and drink.

Cm(Bm)   Ab(G)   Eb(D)

I will praise,— praise, praise— Your name— a-gain.

Cm(Bm)   Ab(G)   (v.2)   Eb(D)

I will rest,— rest, rest,— rest at— Your feet,

Cm(Bm)   Ab(G)   Eb(D)

for You have won— my heart— once a-gain.

1.

2. *Chorus*   Ab(G)

2. I will thirst,—   And You are God,— with

2. I will thirst, thirst, thirst
   For all that You give,
   And I will fall, fall, fall
   Into Your arms again.
   I will call, call, call
   To You alone each day,
   For You have won my heart once again.

3. I shall wait, wait, wait
   At the cross where we meet,
   And I will live, live, live
   By Your name I speak.
   I will run, run, run
   For Your face to seek,
   For You have won my heart once again.

30.
Jesus, all for Jesus
(All for Jesus)

Jennifer Atkinson
& Robin Mark

Steadily

1. Je - sus,_____ all for Je - sus;_____ all I

am and have_____ and ev - er hope to be._____

2nd & Last time *(Fine)* **Repeat v.2**

be. hands. For it's

on - ly in_____ Your will_ that I am free._____ For it's

on - ly in_____ Your will_ that_ I am free.

2. All of my ambitions, hopes and plans,
I surrender these into Your hands.
(Repeat)

31. Jesus, Jesus, Jesus
(Jesus, how I love Your name)

Simply

Dave Bilbrough

Je - sus,___ Je - sus,___ Je - sus,___ ___ how I love Your name.___ The sweet-est song___ on earth___ ___ will ne-ver be e-nough___ to tell the won - der of___ Your___ love. Come hide me in___ Your arms,___ and calm my rest - less heart;___ ___ I hun - ger Lord,___ for, more of___ You.

Event 01/02

32. Jesus, Name above all names

(The Jesus song)

Tenderly

Owen Hurter

Verse

Je - sus, Name a - bove all names,
Je - sus, e - cho - ing through - out

my soul cries Je - sus,
all of the hea - vens, an -

it's the sweet - est song.
ge - lic hosts pro - claim.

Chorus

Morn - ing Star,
Ris - ing Sun, Li - ly of the Val - ley, Rose of Sha -

33.

Jesus, Redeemer
(Redeemer)

Tim Hughes

Rhythmically

Verse

1. Je-sus, Re - deem-er, Friend and King to me.

My re-fuge, my_ com-fort, You're ev-'ry-thing to me._ And this heart is on_ fire for You,_ yes, this heart is on_ fire for You._ For

Chorus

You a-lone are won-der-ful, You a-lone are Coun-sel-lor,

e - ver - last - ing Fa - ther, migh - ty in the hea - vens.

Ne - ver to for - get the love You dis - played up - on a cross,

Son of God I thank You; Prince of Peace, I love Your

name.

2. Saviour, Healer,
Just and true are You.
Now reigning in glory,
Most high and living God.
And this heart is in awe of You,
Yes, this heart is in awe of You.

34.
Jesus taught us how to pray
(Can I see heaven?)

Capo 4 (C)

With energy

James Gregory

Je - sus taught___ us how___ to pray:___
Would You give___ us what___ we need,___

Fa - ther, hal - lowed be___ Your name.
and for - give___ our fool - ish ways?___

I know Je -

sus on - ly prayed,___

Fa - ther, what___ You had___ or - dained.___

Look to the Lord and His strength; seek His face always.

1 CHRONICLES 16:11

35. Knowing Your grace
(Child of the King)

Terry Virgo
& Stuart Townend

Gently

1. Know-ing Your grace has set me free, Lord. I'm
seek-ing Your face; I feel Your plea - sure, Your
joy in the ones You have cho - sen by name. You've
lif - ted my bur - dens and cast off my shame.
I am a child of the King. You will fin - ish the work

Event 01/02

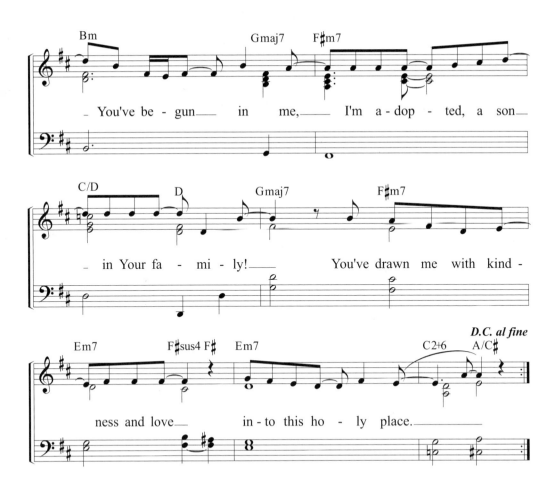

2. Feeling Your touch
   Gives me such peace, Lord.
   I love You so much,
   I know You'll lead me.
   Wherever I go I'll be under Your wing,
   For I am a child of the King.

3. What can I say?
   Your lavish mercy
   Turned night into day -
   My guilt has gone now.
   Forever I'll stand in Your presence and sing,
   For I am a child of the King.

36.

Light of the world
(Here I am)

Capo 2(D)

Tim Hughes

With feeling

1. Light of the world, You stepped down in-to dark - ness,
o - pened my eyes, let me____ see____ beau - ty that made this____
heart a - dore____ You, hope of a life spent with____ You.____

Chorus

So here I am to wor - ship, here I am to
bow down, here I am to say that You're my God.____

Event 01/02

2. King of all days
   Oh so highly exalted,
   Glorious in heaven above.
   Humbly You came
   To the earth You created,
   All for love's sake became poor.

37. Like a fragrant oil

(Fragrant)

Capo 5(D)

Paul Oakley

Tenderly

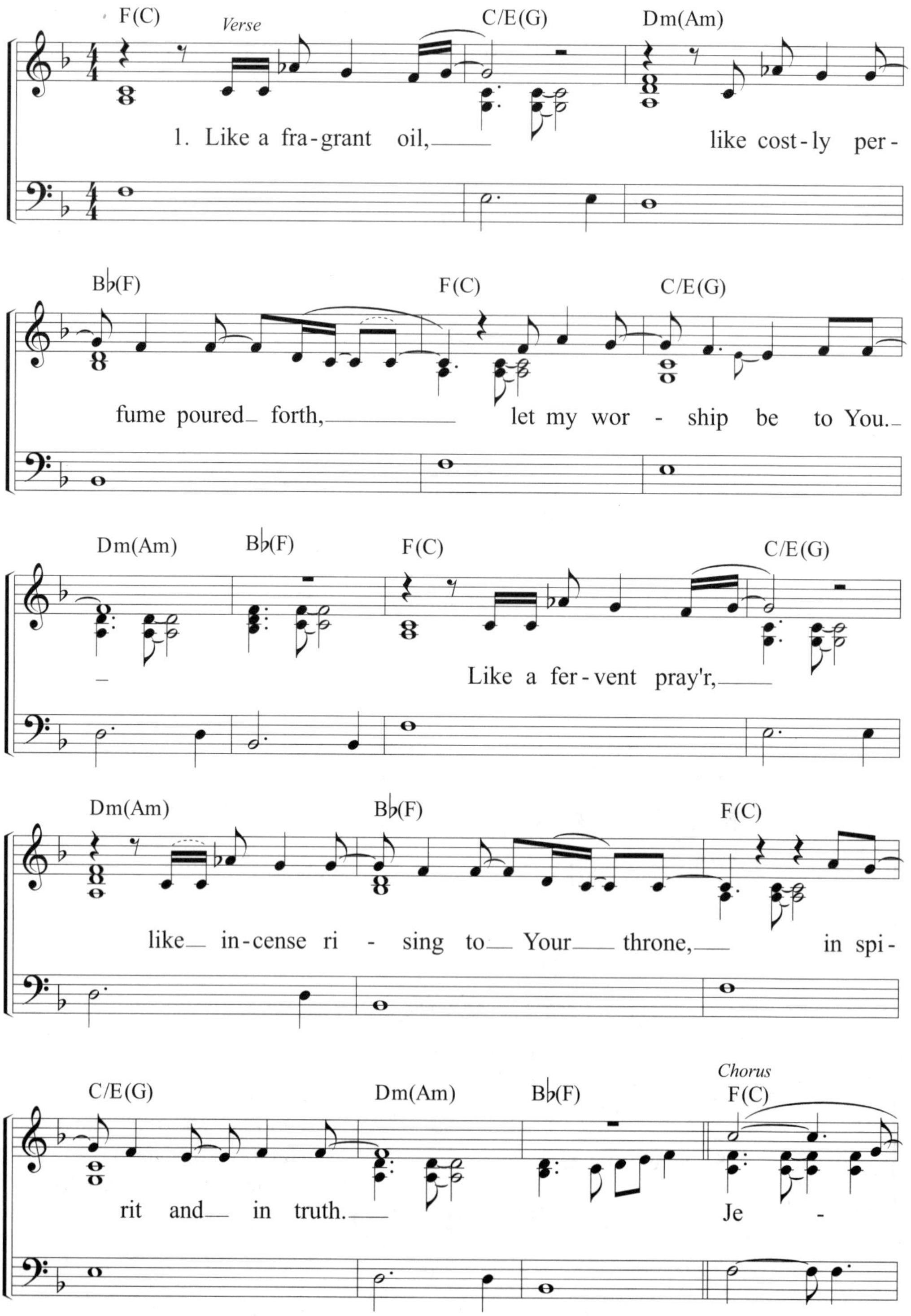

F(C)
Verse
C/E(G)
Dm(Am)
1. Like a fra-grant oil, like cost-ly per-
B♭(F)
F(C)
C/E(G)
fume poured forth, let my wor - ship be to You.
Dm(Am)
B♭(F)
F(C)
C/E(G)
Like a fer-vent pray'r,
Dm(Am)
B♭(F)
F(C)
like in-cense ri - sing to Your throne, in spi-
C/E(G)
Dm(Am)
B♭(F)
Chorus
F(C)
rit and in truth. Je -

Event 01/02

2. Like a wedding vow,
   'All I am I give to You,'
   Let my sacrifice be pure.
   Like the sweetest sound,
   Like a lover's whisper in your ear,
   I've set my heart on You.

38. Look what You've done in my life
(Your love)

Eoghan Heaslip
& M. Goss

Steady 4

Verse

Look what You've done in my life,
see what You've done in this heart;____ You've brought hope,
heal-ing and free - dom, look what You've done in my life.____
And though I'm not de-serv - ing of____ Your____
love, You give it all____ to me,____ with o - pen arms____

39. Lord, You are my righteousness

Andrew Rogers

Steadily

1. Lord, You are my right - eous - ness, the
2. Though You are the King of kings,

One who sanc - ti - fies my life, my Shep - herd and my
yet You are my next of kin, and my near - est

guide. Ban - ner of de - li - ve - rance,
friend. Lay - ing down Your life for me,

war - ri - or and my de - fence, in Your se - cret place I hide.
Your a - ma - zing grace I see, and Your love with - out an end.

Ev - 'ry o - ther throne must fall
How can I keep si - lent, Lord?

Event 01/02

40.   May the words of my mouth

Tim Hughes
& Rob Hill

Event 01/02

I will fol-low, I will fol-low, I will fol-low You.

I will fol-low You. For this— is what

You.

2. Lord, will You be my vision,
   Lord, will You be my guide?
   Be my hope, be my light and the way.
   And I'll look not for riches,
   Nor praises on earth,
   Only You'll be the first of my heart.

But because of His great love for us, God, who is rich in mercy, made us alive with Christ even when we were dead in transgressions – it is by grace you have been saved.

EPHESIANS 2:4-5

41. More than I could hope or dream of
(One day)

With energy

Reuben Morgan

More than I could hope or dream of,

You have poured Your fa-vour on me.— One day in the

house of— God is bet-ter than a thou-sand days in the world.—

So— blessed,

I can't con-tain— it,— so— much I've got to give it a-way.—

Event 01/02

He gives strength to the weary and increases the power of the weak. Even youths grow tired and weary, and young men stumble and fall; but those who hope in the Lord will renew their strength. They will soar on wings like eagles; they will run and not grow weary, they will walk and not faint.

ISAIAH 40:29-31

42. My hope is in the Lord

Simply

Robin Mark

is come.＿ For＿ I＿ ＿ is come,＿

that the hope＿＿ of my＿ heart＿

is come.＿＿

43.

My hope rests firm

With feeling

Keith Getty
& Richard Creighton

1. My hope rests firm on Jesus Christ, He is my only plea: though all the world should point and scorn, His ransom leaves me free, His ransom leaves me free.

Event 01/02

Last time

2. My—

2. My hope sustains me as I strive
   And strain towards the goal;
   Though I still stumble into sin,
   His death paid for it all,
   His death paid for it all.

3. My hope provides me with a spur
   To help me run this race:
   I know my tears will turn to joy
   The day I see His face,
   The day I see His face.

4. My hope is to be with my Lord,
   To know as I am known:
   To serve Him gladly all my days
   In praise before His throne,
   In praise before His throne.

44.

Name above all names

Capo 3(D)

Neil Bennetts

Worshipfully

1. Name a-bove all names, the Sa-viour for sin--ners slain. You suf-fered for my sake, to bring me back home a-gain. When I was lost You poured your life out for me. Name a-bove all names, Je-sus, I love You.

Event 01/02

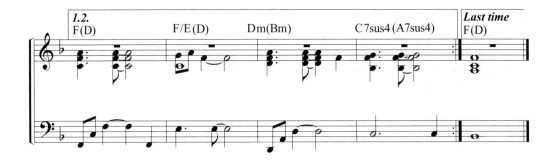

2. Giver of mercy,
   The fountain of life for me.
   My spirit is lifted
   To soar on the eagle's wings.
   What love is this
   That fills my heart with treasure?
   Name above all names,
   Jesus, I love You.

3. High King eternal,
   The one true and faithful God.
   The beautiful Saviour,
   Still reigning in power and love.
   With all my heart
   I'll worship You forever:
   Name above all names,
   Jesus, I love You.

45. Nothing is too much to ask

Matt Redman
& Mike Pilavachi

Gently, building with each section

No - thing is too much to ask, now that I have said I'm Yours. Je-sus, take the whole of me un - re - serv - ed - ly. Je-sus take me deep - er now, that I might go fur - ther too, I've re - ceived so much from You,

46.

Oh fallen one

(Arise)

James Gregory

With strength

1. Oh fal-len one ___ co-vered now ___ in shame, ___ He is your hope, ___ He is your life. Though He should judge, ___ His an-ger turns ___ a - way; ___ rise from the dust, beau-ti-ful one. ___ A -

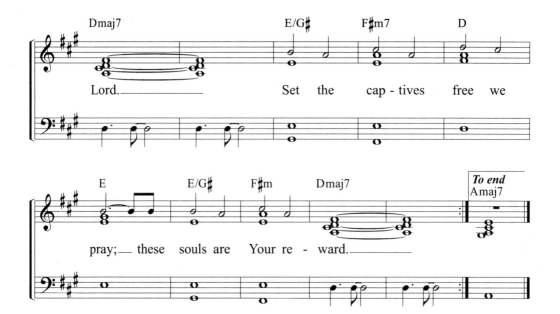

Lord. _____ Set the cap - tives free we pray; ___ these souls are Your re - ward. _____

2. Don't be afraid,
   For you're not left alone;
   His heart of love is broken for you.
   Your Father cares
   For all your children now,
   Arise in His name, beautiful one.

3. Lift up your eyes,
   Many come to see
   The splendour your God has given to you.
   Could each of your saints
   Become a thousand saints?
   Rise up and praise, beautiful one.

47.

O Lord, when I wake up

(Lift high)

Brian Houston

1. O Lord,————— when I wake—— up in the morn - ing, let my
   ——— when I go—— out in the eve - ning, let my

mouth be filled with praise for You.—— O Lord,— – that
mouth be filled with praise for You,—

all might know,— yeah,——— and ma-ny might see— yeah,—

— that You're my Lord.————————

Bridge

Fill me with a spi - rit of bold-ness, oh my God,————

2. O Lord, when I'm stressed and feeling tired,
Let my mouth be filled with praise to You.
O Lord, when I'm pressed on every side,
Let my mouth be filled with praise to You.
That all might know and many might see
That You are Lord.

Fill me with a spirit of boldness. . .

48.

Only You
(Nothing compares to You)

James Taylor

Medium pace

1. On-ly You____ can re-place____ rags for rich-
(2.) ____ de-mons flee,____ moun-tains trem-

es pure____ as gold,____ and Your mer-
ble in Your sight,____ but You love-

cy saved____ my soul,____ there's none like You.
_ me like____ a friend,____

1.3. E / B / *2.4.* E

2. At Your name_ _

Chorus / D

No - thing com-pares____ to You,____

3. You have paid such a cost,
   So much more than can be won:
   God, You gave Your only Son,
   There's none like You.

4. So we'll bow to the cross
   Where the tears of heaven fall,
   You have heard the sinner's call:
   There's none like You.

49.
Open the eyes of my heart

Simply

Paul Baloche

ho - ly, ho - ly, ho - ly.

D.C.

Ho - ly, ho - ly, ho - ly,— ho - ly, ho - ly, ho -

ly,— ho - ly, ho - ly, ho - ly,— I want to see— You.—

to fade

50. Salvation, spring up
(Salvation)

With excitement

Charlie Hall

Sal-va-tion, spring up from the ground, Lord, rend the heav-ens and come down. Seek the lost and heal the lame; Je-sus bring glo-ry to Your name. Let all the prod-i-gals run home, all of cre-a-tion waits and groans. Lord, we've heard

(Fine)

_ of Your_ great fame; Fa -ther, cause all to shout_ Your name.

N.C.

B   C#m   A

Stir up our hearts,____ O___ God;____

B   C#m   A

‘ o - pen our spir - its to awe___ who You are.___

After this I heard what sounded like the roar of a great multitude in heaven shouting: "Hallelujah! Salvation and glory and power belong to our God, for true and just are His judgements.

REVELATION 19:1-2

51. Sing praises to our God

David Lyle Morris

Sing prai-ses to our God, sing prai-ses.

Sing prai-ses to the King, sing prai-ses. (For)

God is King of all the earth, sing to Him a psalm of praise.

God reigns o-ver the na-tions, all our wor-ship we will raise.

He's King of all the earth, bring to Him a joy-ful song.

Event 01/02

52. Spirit move on this land
(Revival in our land)

Tim Sherrington

With a rock feel

Spi-rit move on this land,

take Your peo - ple in Your hands.

We're wait - ing for the day,

the day You come a-gain.

Your Spi-rit is com-ing to give to the poor;

Event 01/02

53.

Standing on holy ground
(Isaiah 12)

With awe

Paul Oakley
& Martin Cooper

Lyrics:
Stand-ing on ho-ly ground, mer-cy and grace I've found. I'm here be-fore Your throne now, by a new and liv-ing way. Je-sus I come to You, I lift up my eyes to You.

54.
Teach me of Your ways
(Lord, have Your way)

Capo 2 (G)

David Gate

1. Teach me of Your ways, to hon - our You with all I have, and that I learn to say: 'Not my will but Yours, my Lord.' O Je - sus,

2. Lord I long to be
   A faithful child who honours You,
   So Jesus be in me,
   Let Your light shine through me now.

55.

The place where You dwell

Ed Pask

Gentle 3

1. The place where You dwell⏤ is where I⏤ want to be,⏤

⏤ it's where an-gels in splen - dour⏤ wor-ship the King.⏤

⏤ And to Je-sus in glo-ry each voice raised in song:

ho - ly, ho - ly, ho - ly is the Lord.⏤

2. In the   It's all for You,⏤

Event 01/02

2. In the light of Your presence
   I find perfect peace,
   And my heart shall adore You
   And in You rejoice.
   And to Jesus victorious
   I lift up my song:
   Worthy, worthy, worthy is the Lamb.

56.
There is a day

Nathan Fellingham

1.
There is a day— that all cre - a - tion's wait - ing for,—
a day of free - dom— and li - be - ra - tion from— the earth.—

And on that day,— the Lord will come to meet— His bride.—
And when we see— Him, in an in - stant we'll be changed.—

(To verse 2)

Chorus
We will meet— Him in the air— and then we—

Event 01/02

will be like Him, for we will see Him as He is, oh yeah! Then all hurt and pain will cease, and we'll be with Him for-e-ver, and in His glo-ry we will live. Oh yeah, oh yeah!

D.C. (v.3)

2. The trumpet sounds and the dead will then be raised
   By His power, never to perish again.
   Once only flesh, now clothed with immortality;
   Death has now been swallowed up in victory.

3. So lift your eyes to the things as yet unseen,
   That will remain now for all eternity.
   Though trouble's hard, it's only momentary,
   And it's achieving our future glory.

57.

There is a name
(High over all)

Nathan Fellingham

With energy

1. There is a name that's high o-ver all.

There is a King seat-ed on— the throne.

And He's in - ter-ced - ing for— me,

so that I— will be— made ho - ly,

2. There is a Man who walked on the earth,
   The Word of God made known to us.
   He's the image of the Father,
   The Firstborn over creation,
   Yet He suffered at the hands of those He saves.

58.

There's a call
(We will go)

Stuart Townend

Verse 1:
There's a call to the peo-ple of Zi-on, to a-rise and pos-sess the land;— ev-'ry town has its heirs to the pro-mise, ev-'ry na-tion its sons of light.—

Verse 2:
We have stayed long e-nough on this moun-tain, now we're called to new realms of faith;— we are more than a tem-ple of wor-ship, we're an ar-my of praise!—

We will go— to ev-'ry place, shar-ing mer — cy and preach-ing grace,— for the

2. We have drunk of the wine of His presence,
   We have feasted upon His word;
   Now we're hungry for works of power,
   Now we're thirsty to share His love.
   He will give us the ground that we walk on,
   For the battle belongs to God;
   Do not fear, for His grace is sufficient,
   When we're weak, He is strong!

Humble yourselves before the Lord, and He will lift you up.

JAMES 4:10

59. We fall down

Intensely

Chris Tomlin

We fall down, we lay our crowns at the feet of Je-
-sus. The great-ness of mer-cy and love, at the feet
of Je - sus. And we cry ho - ly, ho - ly, ho - ly. And we cry
ho - ly, ho - ly, ho - ly. And we cry ho - ly, ho - ly, ho-
- ly is the Lamb.

Event 01/02

60. We're gonna sing like the saved
(Sing like the saved)

Energetic and funky

Matt Redman

We're gon-na sing like the saved.

We're gon-na sing like the saved.

We're gon-na sing like the saved.

Last time to Coda

We're gon-na sing like the saved. It is our du-

ty and our joy, in ev-'ry time and ev-'ry place,

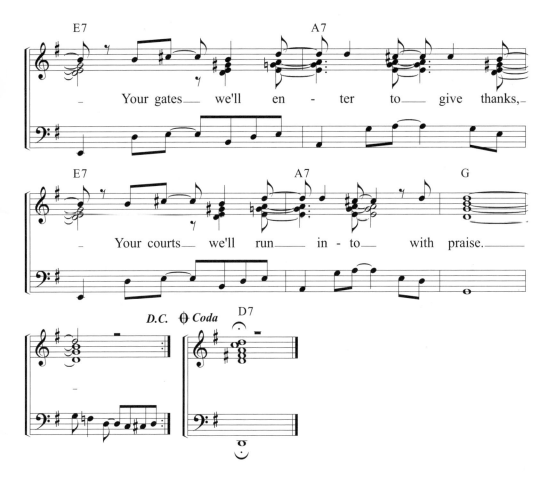

Your gates — we'll en - ter to — give thanks, —

Your courts — we'll run — in - to — with praise. —

D.C. ✛ *Coda*

2. A joyful noise we will make . . .

3. You put Your joy in our hearts . . .

4. We're gonna dance like the saved . . .

61.
We've come to praise You

Capo 3(D)

Gospel feel

Kate Simmonds
& Stuart Townend

We've come— to praise— You, 'cause You're wor -
thy. No - bo - dy like— You in Your glo -
ry. We love— to praise— You, 'cause You're ho -
ly, awe - some, won - der-ful, migh-ty God.

(repeat 1st time only)
(Fine)

And e - v'ry-thing that You do— comes from a heart—

Event 01/02

will He freely give to us who call up-on His name,

who call up-on His name, who

call up-on His name, who call up-on His name?

D.C. al fine

62.

What to say, Lord?
(Every day)

With life

Joel Houston

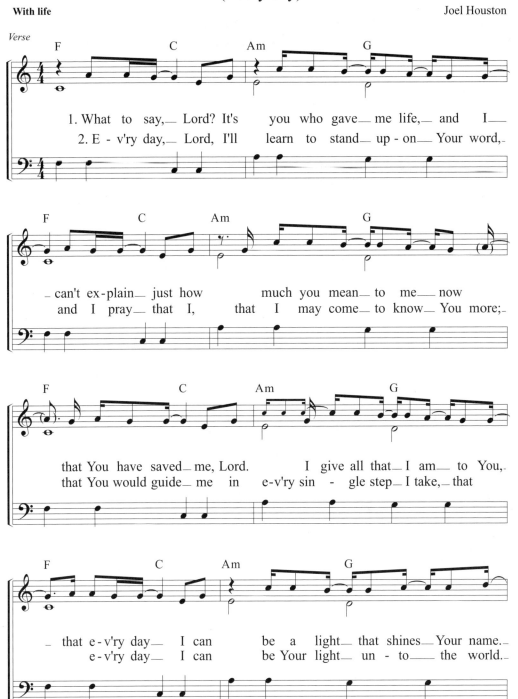

Verse

1. What to say,— Lord? It's you who gave— me life,— and I— can't ex-plain— just how much you mean— to me— now that You have saved— me, Lord. I give all that— I am— to You,— that e-v'ry day— I can be a light— that shines— Your name.—

2. E-v'ry day,— Lord, I'll learn to stand— up-on— Your word,— and I pray— that I, that I may come— to know— You more;— that You would guide— me in e-v'ry sin - gle step— I take,— that e-v'ry day— I can be Your light— un-to— the world.—

Event 01/02

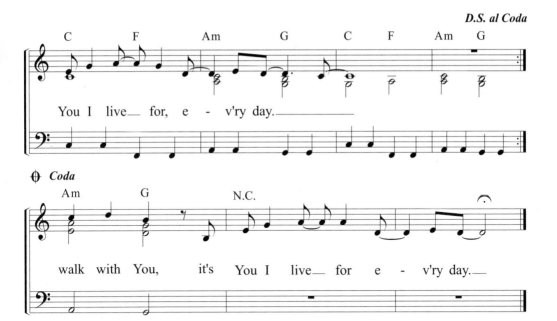

D.S. al Coda

You I live— for, e - v'ry day.—————————

Coda

walk with You, it's You I live— for e - v'ry day.——

63.
What can I say?

Capo 3(D)

Neil Bennetts

Steadily

What can I say,____ but 'I love____ You'?____ What can I
do,____ but to bow____ down?____ What can I

say,____ but 'I praise____ You'?____ As the train of Your robe____ fills this tem-
do,____ but to wor - ship?____ On - ly You are the One____ who is wor-

ple,____ as the sound of Your voice____ fills this place.____ What can I
thy,____ on - ly

1.

You are the One____ who is Lord.____ Great is the Lord,____

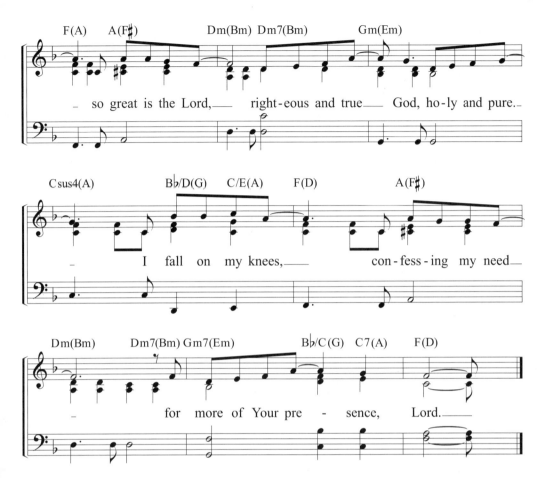

64.

When I survey
(The wonderful cross)

Isaac Watts (1674-1748)
Arrangement by Jesse Reeves and Chris Tomlin
Refrain lyrics by Chris Tomlin and J.D. Walt

Somberly

1. When I sur-vey the___ won-drous___ cross on which the Prince of___ Glo-ry___ died, my rich-est gain I___ count but___ loss, and pour con-tempt on all my___ pride.

1. crown? Oh, the won-der-ful cross,___ oh, the

Event 01/02

2. See from His head, His hands, His feet,
   Sorrow and love flow mingled down;
   Did e'er such love and sorrow meet,
   Or thorns compose so rich a crown?

2. Were the whole realm of nature mine,
   That were an offering far too small.
   Love so amazing, so divine,
   Demands my soul, my life, my all.

65.

When Love came down

Stuart Townend

Tenderly

1. When Love came down to earth and made His home with men, the hope-less found a hope, the sin-ner found a friend. Not to the pow-er-ful but to the poor He came, and hum-ble, hun-gry hearts were sa-tis-fied a-gain. *Chorus* What joy, what peace has come to us! What

Event 01/02

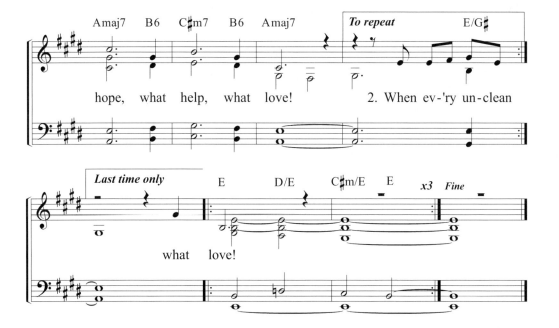

hope, what help, what love!   2. When ev-'ry un-clean

what love!

2. When every unclean thought,
   And every sinful deed
   Was scourged upon His back
   And hammered through His feet.
   The Innocent is cursed,
   The guilty are released;
   The punishment of God
   On God has bought me peace.

3. Come lay your heavy load
   Down at the Master's feet;
   Your shame will be removed,
   Your joy will be complete.
   Come crucify your pride,
   And enter as a child;
   For those who bow down low
   He'll lift up to His side.

66.

When I was lost

(There is a new song)

Capo 3(D)

Gospel feel

Kate & Miles Simmonds

1. When I was lost, You came and res-cued me;
reached down in-to the pit and lif-ted me.
O Lord, such love, I was as far from You as
I could be.

You know all the things I've e-ver done,
but Je-sus' blood has can-celled e-v'ry one.
O Lord, such grace to qua-li-
fy me as Your own.

Chorus

There is a new song in my mouth, there is a
stand firm on this Rock, my life is-

_ have planned.___ How beau-ti-ful___ the grace___ that gives_ _ to us___ all that we don't___ de-serve,_____ all that we can- not earn,___ but is a gift___ of love.___ Your love has lif-ted me. There is a me.

2. Now I have come into Your family,
For the Son of God has died for me.
Oh Lord, such peace,
I am as loved by You as I could be.
In the full assurance of Your love,
Now with every confidence we come.
O Lord, such joy
To know that You delight in us.

67.
When we turn our hearts to heaven
(Dreamers of Your dreams)

Capo 3(G)

Quietly rhythmic

Noel Richards
& Ken Riley

When we turn —— our hearts — to hea - ven and — bow down, —

we'll see fa - thers and — the chil -

dren re - con - ciled. —— We'll be — the drea -

mers of —— Your dreams. ——

68. Who can compare?

Gareth Robinson

1. Who can com-pare— with You, my Fa - ther; lo-ving and kind,—
faith-ful and true?— When You for-give— my heart that is bro - ken, I
grate-ful-ly sing— my love to You.— I wor - ship
You, I love_____ You:

2. Here I will dwell in the arms of my Father,
   Knowing Your grace, hearing Your voice.
   Trusting Your word, feeling Your peace,
   Resting in You and in Your love.

69.

Who's the only light?

(It's all about Jesus)

Scott Underwood

Steadily

1. Who's the on - ly light___ that shines and ne-ver fades?___

The Light___ of the world,___ Je-sus.

Who's the on - ly light___ that drives the dark___ a-way?___

The Light___ of the world,___ Je-sus. It's all___ a-bout

Chorus

Je-sus,___ Je-sus, it's all___ a-bout Je-sus,___

Event 01/02

2. Who's the only Word that made all things?
   The Word was God, Jesus.
   He's the only truth, the fullness of the Lord,
   The Son of God, Jesus.

70.

Worship the Lord

Louise Fellingham

Rock feel

Verse

1. Wor - ship— the Lord,— see the splen - dour of— His ho - li - ness.— Give— to— the Lord— all the glo - ry due— His name.—

Come and— a - dore,— come and lay Your hearts— be - fore— Him. With thank - ful - ness— and love,— come and shout a - loud— Your praise.—

Chorus

De - clare His glo - ry a - mong all— the na-

2. We are His people, belonging to our Father,
   Set apart for truth, we are chosen by God.
   With confidence we come, we are free and we're forgiven.
   Blessed are the ones who put their hope in God.

3. Please come upon us now, we want to see Your face, Lord.
   Soften our hearts, take us deeper into You.
   Spirit, fill our minds with the knowledge of Your wisdom.
   Come and touch our mouths, help us tell of all You've done.

71.
You are all I want

Gareth Robinson

Brightly

1. You are all I want,— You're all I need— to be set free.—
Your cross of death— gives life to me,— Your sa - cri - fice—
brings li - ber - ty.— No one else could take—
my place but You,— the per - fect One,— the ho - ly God,—
re - vealed as man— in Je - sus Christ.—

Event 01/02

2. I will give to You my everything,
   Abandon all my selfish dreams
   To live for You and do Your will every day.
   You have touched my heart and made me whole,
   You've made me clean, so I will give
   My offering of love to You,
   All my life lived just for You, 'cause...

72.

You are my anchor

With a steady rock feel

Stuart Townend

Verse

1. You are my an - chor,— my light and my sal-
va - tion. You are my re - fuge,— my heart will not fear.— Though my foes— sur - round— me on ev - 'ry hand,— they will stum - ble and fall— while in grace— I stand.— In my day—

Event 01/02

2. Teach me Your way,——

2. Teach me Your way, Lord,
   Make straight the path before me.
   Do not forsake me,
   My hope is in You.
   As I walk through life, I am confident
   I will see Your goodness with every step,
   And my heart directs me to seek You in all that I do,
   So I will wait for You.

Blessed are those who hunger and thirst for righteousness, for they will be filled.

MATTHEW 5:6

73.
You are the One

Sue Rinaldi
& Caroline Bonnett

You are the One I love,___ You are the One that I___ a - dore.___

1. For You've called___ me by___ name, drawn me close___ to Your___ heart, washed a - way___ all my___ shame___ with Your tears.___ For the rest___ of my___ days,___

I will of - fer my life in thanks-giv - ing and praise to my King. Such pre - cious, pre - cious love. You have won me with Your

2. Now with You I will stay,
   For Your word is my light,
   And Your peace can allay all my fears;
   And my victory song
   Is the song of the cross,
   You have won me with love so divine.

74.

You call us first
(One thing)

Capo 5(C)

Worshipfully

Luke 10:41
Tim Hughes

1. You call us first to love Your name,
2. Your ho - nour, Lord, Your name's re - nown

— to wor - ship You. To please Your heart
— we long to see. So let the glo -

— our one de - sire, O Lord.
ry of Your name be praised.

Chorus

If there's one thing we are called to do, it's to love You, to a-

Event 01/02

75.
You can have my whole life

Worshipful

James Taylor

You can have my whole— life, You can come— and have— it— all:—

I don't want— to go— my own— way now.—

I love to feel Your pre-

- sence and I know— Your sav - ing— grace,— I am no-

- thing when— You're se - cond place.—

Event 01/02

Delight yourself in the Lord and He will give you the desires of your heart.

PSALM 37:4

76.

You pour out grace

Gareth Robinson

Steadily

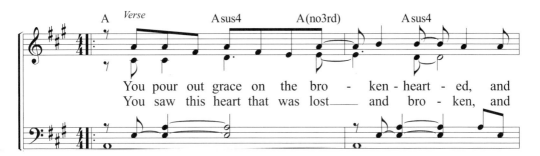

You pour out grace on the bro - ken - heart - ed, and
You saw this heart that was lost____ and bro - ken, and

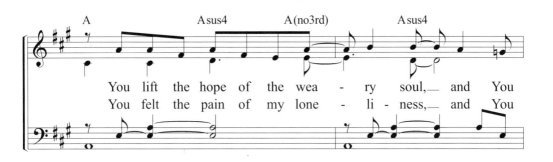

You lift the hope of the wea - ry soul,____ and You
You felt the pain of my lone - li - ness,____ and You

stretch out Your hand with Your lov - ing mer - cy.
be - friend - ed me and re - stored____

1. D

2. D

____ my dig - ni - ty.____

Event 01/02

77. Your face outshines the brightest sun
(King of glory)

With strength

Matt Redman
& David Gate

Verse

face— out - shines— the bright - est sun,
eyes— that— blaze— like burn - ing fire,

Je - sus,— You're glor - i - ous. You— are— so

glor - i - ous.— With

2. Your voice like rushing waters sounds,
   Jesus You're powerful, You are so powerful.
   And in Your hands You hold the stars,
   Jesus You're powerful, You are so powerful.

78.

Your hand, O God, has guided

(One church)

Capo 3 (D)

Music: Keith Getty

Steadily

1. Your— hand, O God, has— gui - ded Your—

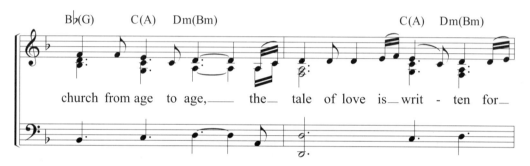

church from age to age,— the— tale of love is—writ - ten for—

us on e - v'ry page. Our fa - thers knew— Your— good - ness, and

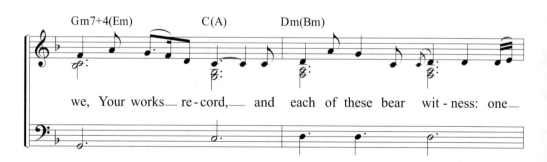

we, Your works— re - cord,— and each of these bear wit - ness: one—

Event 01/02

2. Your mercy never fails us, or leaves Your work undone;
   With Your right hand to help us, the victory shall be won.
   And then with heaven's angels Your name shall be adored,
   And they shall praise You, singing: one church, one faith, one Lord.

E. H. Plumptre (1821-91) adpt. Keith Getty.

79.
Your kingdom generation
(Here to eternity)

Steadily

Darlene Zschech
& David Moyse

Your king - dom ge - ne-ra - tion de-clares___ Your ma-

- je-sty,___ and our lives___ are___ re - sound - ing with___ Your praise.

We see___ Your Spi - rit mov - ing,

we burn with ho - ly fi - re. Your glo - ry___ is

seen through all_____ the earth._____

Event 01/02

we'll take our place in hi - sto-ry.___ We'll shout Your awe-

some love___ from here___ to___ e-ter - ni-ty.___

80.

Your love is amazing
(Hallelujah)

Steadily

Brian Doerksen
& Brenton Brown

1.(3.) Your love is a-maz - ing, stea-dy and un-chang-

- ing; Your love is a moun - tain firm be-neath my feet.

- Your love is a mys - t'ry, how you gent - ly lift

- me; when I am sur-round - ed, Your love car - ries me.

Chorus

Hal-le-lu - jah, hal-le-lu - jah, hal-le-lu-

Event 01/02

Lord, You make me sing,

how You make me sing.

2. Your love is surprising,
   I can feel it rising,
   All the joy that's growing deep inside of me.
   Every time I see You,
   All your goodness shines through,
   I can feel this God song
   Rising up in me.

81.

Your love is better than wine

(Draw me after You)

Robert Critchley

Event 01/02

82.

Your whisper to my soul

Brian Houston

Country rock feel

Your whis - per to my soul
when I was like a child, lift - ed off the yoke,
plan - ted fields of hope in this heart of mine.

You took me as I am,
You knew what I had done, still You took my shame.
and You called my name, I was o - ver - come.

When You broke the bonds of how I used to be,

You rolled a-way the stone, You set the cap-tive free.

83.

You set me apart
(Dwell in Your house)

Paul Ewing

Steadily

1. You set me a-part,— gave— me a new heart,

filled with com-pas - sion to share— Your great love.

Show me Your way,— I— want to know— You.

Guide me in truth,— my hope— is in You.—

Chorus

That I may— dwell in— Your— house— for-e - ver,

Event 01/02

Sweet a-noint - ing teach— our— hearts,———— our lives,— we———— pray.———————— That I may— dwell in— Your— house— for - e - ver— more.———

2. I'll hold on to You,
   My Strength and my Refuge.
   Whom shall I fear?
   I know You are near.
   All of my days
   I live for You, Lord.
   Establish my path,
   There's one thing I ask.

84. You shaped the heavens
(Maker of all things)

Jer 10:16, Col 1:16-17,
Ps 19:1

Tim Hughes

Strongly

1. You shaped the hea-vens and the earth, re-vealed Your splen - dour. You spoke Your life in-to our hearts, so we be-long to You.

Chorus

You are the Mak-er of all things, First and the Last, cre-a-tion sings praise

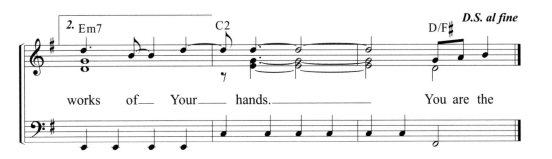

2. Em7   C2   D/F♯   **D.S. al fine**

works   of__   Your____   hands._____   You are the

          2. Creator God, in You all things
             Now hold together.
             Working Your wonders day by day,
             You'll reign forever.

85. You take me by the hand
(Carry me)

Dave Bilbrough

Event 01/02

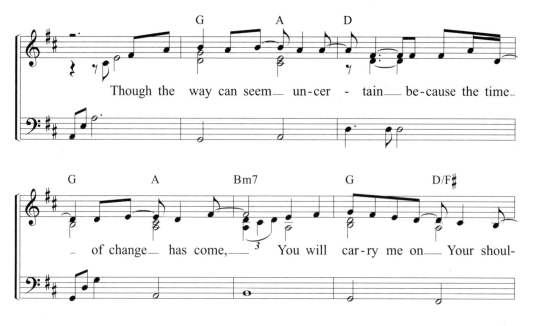

Though the way can seem__ un-cer - tain__ be-cause the time__

__ of change__ has come,__ You will car-ry me on__ Your shoul-

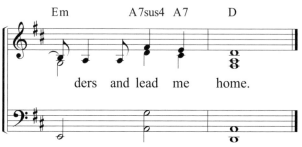

ders and lead me home.

ACETATES/WORDS SECTION

For use by worship leaders, singers and guitarists
(who may wish to write guitar chords above the words).

Those with a Church Copyright Licence can
also photocopy these pages onto acetate
to use with overhead projectors.

The following pages,
if enlarged by a factor of 125%
should fit A4-size acetates.

A humble heart You have yet to despise,
And so I humble myself in this place.
If they that sow in tears shall reap in joy,
Let a million tears or more roll down my
        face.
If You don't answer me today, Lord,
I'm gonna be right here tomorrow.
If You don't answer when I pray
From the morning to the evening,
'Cause it's You I do believe in,
I will say, every day, I'm gonna say that…

I won't let go till You bless me, Lord,
No, I won't let go till You bless me, Lord.
And I will cry out to You
Till I can't cry no more.
And I won't let go till You bless me, Lord.

Brian Houston
Copyright © 2000 Kingsway's Thankyou Music, P.O. Box 75,
Eastbourne, East Sussex, BN23 6NW, UK. tym@kingsway.co.uk.

CCL licence no. _____

Where can I go if You don't bid me go?
And I have no hope if You are not my hope.
And I have no peace if You don't give me
    peace,
And I have no faith if You don't help me to
    believe.
If You don't answer me today
Will the heathen nations mock Your name
And say You're made of wood or clay?
Ah, but I've seen You provide for me,
I've kissed Your lips and felt You heal my
    pain.
Hey, can You do it once again? 'Cause…

I won't let go till You bless me, Lord,
No, I won't let go till You bless me, Lord.
And I will cry out to You
Till I can't cry no more.
And I won't let go till You bless me, Lord.

All of me,
All of me, I give to You,
Only You, Jesus.
More of You,
More of You I long for,
Only You, Jesus.

For this life I live for You.
I truly worship You,
All of my days, in every way.
I will praise You
In thought and word and deed,
Powered by Your life in me.
All of my days, in every way
I will praise You, Lord.

Gareth Robinson
Copyright © 2001 Kingsway's Thankyou Music, P.O. Box 75,
Eastbourne, East Sussex, BN23 6NW, UK. tym@kingsway.co.uk.

CCL licence no. _____

Almighty God, faithful and true,
In my worship I want to meet with You.
Unchanging God, forever the same,
It's You I worship,
To know Your heart again.

And I fall down on my knees again,
As You show me what grace means;
And You love with such amazing love,
O my God, how can this be?

Mark Vargeson
Copyright © 2001 Kingsway's Thankyou Music, P.O. Box 75,
Eastbourne, East Sussex, BN23 6NW, UK. tym@kingsway.co.uk.

And after all,
Everything I once held dear
Just proved to be so vain.
To lose it all,
And find a Friend who's always near
Could only be my gain.
And when I think of what You've done for
    me,
To bring me to the Father's side:

Unashamed and unafraid,
I will choose to wear Your name,
In a world so full of hate,
I will always live Your way.

Could it be
That You should put on human flesh,
Your glory laid aside?
Bruised for me,
Majesty upon the cross,
Forsaken and despised.
When I think of what it cost for You,
To bring me to the Father's side:

Unashamed and unafraid,
I will choose to wear Your name,
In a world so full of hate,
I will always live Your way.
Unashamed and unafraid,
I will love You all my days,
I don't care what people say,
I'm unashamed and unfraid.

I know some will say it's foolishness:
You can't make a blind man see.
But I know that there is power in the cross
To save those who believe.

And I'm forgiven,
Because You were forsaken.
And I'm accepted: You were condemned.
And I'm alive and well,
Your Spirit is within me,
Because You died and rose again.

Amazing love, how can it be
That You, my King, would die for me?
Amazing love, I know it's true;
Now it's my joy to honour You.
In all I do, I honour You.

You are my King, You are my King,
Jesus, You are my King,
You are my King.

Billy James Foote
Copyright © 1999 worshiptogether.com songs/EMI Christian Music Publishing/
Adm. by CopyCare, P.O. Box 77, Hailsham, East Sussex, BN27 3EF, UK.
music@copycare.com.

Beauty for ashes and garments of praise,
You come and adorn me with joy once
    again.
And pour oil of gladness instead of despair,
Bringing Your mercy again,
Like sweet spring rain.

Sweet spring rain, mercy from heaven,
Sweet spring rain, come fall down on me.
Jesus, Your truth has come to restore me
In mercy, in mercy.

Neil Bennetts
Copyright © 2000 Daybreak Music Ltd, Silverdale Road,
Eastbourne, East Sussex, BN20 7AB, UK.

Breathe on me, O wind of change,
Anoint me with fresh oil from Your throne.
Lord, restore me with new life,
So I'm ready to serve
And I'm ready to go,
Ready to do Your will.
So I'm ready to serve
And I'm ready to go,
Ready to do Your will.

Lord, help me to run this race
And to live by Your grace,
All I want to do is Your will.

Ready to serve, ready to go,
Ready to do, ready to be,
Ready to do Your will.

Andrea Lawrence & Noel Robinson
Copyright © 2000 Kingsway's Thankyou Music, P.O. Box 75,
Eastbourne, East Sussex, BN23 6NW, UK. tym@kingsway.co.uk.

Come, let us worship the King of kings,
The Creator of all things,
Let your soul arise to Him,
Come and bless the Lord our King.

Lord, my heart and voice I raise,
To praise Your wondrous ways,
And with confidence I come
To approach Your heavenly throne.

Come and fill this place with Your glory,
Come and captivate our gaze;
Come and fill us with Your fire,
That the world might know Your name.

(For) You are God,
And You're worthy to be praised,
And You are good,
For Your love will never end:
The great I Am,
You are faithful in all of Your ways.
(Repeat)

Nathan Fellingham
Copyright © 2001 Kingsway's Thankyou Music, P.O. Box 75,
Eastbourne, East Sussex, BN23 6NW, UK. tym@kingsway.co.uk.

CCL licence no. _____

Come near to God and He
will come near to you.

JAMES 4:8

Give thanks to the Lord,
Our God and King:
His love endures forever.
For He is good, He is above all things.
His love endures forever.
Sing praise, sing praise.

With a mighty hand
And an outstretched arm
His love endures forever.
For the life that's been reborn.
His love endures forever.
Sing praise, sing praise,
Sing praise, sing praise.

Forever, God is faithful,
Forever God is strong.
Forever God is with us,
Forever, forever.

From the rising to the setting sun,
His love endures forever.
By the grace of God, we will carry on.
His love endures forever.
Sing praise, sing praise,
Sing praise, sing praise.

Chris Tomlin
Copyright © 2000 worshiptogether.com songs/Six Steps Music/EMI Christian
Music Publishing/Adm. by CopyCare, P.O. Box 77, Hailsham, East Sussex,
BN27 3EF, UK. music@copycare.com.

CCL licence no. _____

God is our Father in heaven above,
And He cares for His children
With infinite love.
Our worries are needless,
Look up in the sky
Where carefree and singing
The birds freely fly.

Their Maker who knows them,
Supplies all their food,
How much more is our Father
Concerned for our good?

For our Father in heaven
Knows all of our needs,
He will care for us always,
We surrender our all,
And make the kingdom of heaven our goal.

David Lyle Morris & Nick Wynne Jones
Copyright © 2000 Kingsway's Thankyou Music, P.O. Box 75,
Eastbourne, East Sussex, BN23 6NW, UK. tym@kingsway.co.uk.

CCL licence no. _____

Look at the lilies
And see how they grow:
They are clothed by God's goodness
In beautiful show.
Our Father in heaven
Who cares for each flower,
Provides for us always
So great is His power.

The kingdom of heaven
And His righteousness
We will seek with a passion
So all may be blessed.

For our Father in heaven
Knows all of our needs,
He will care for us always,
We surrender our all,
And make the kingdom of heaven our goal.

Good and gracious,
Attributes of a loving Father,
You're high and mighty,
But humble all the same.
You have made the heavens and the earth,
And You made us in Your image, Lord.

Holy, holy, holy is the Lord Almighty,
And we rejoice in You alone,
For You are worthy.
And You have given life to me,
And I love to worship at Your feet,
And I love to love You just for who You are.

Death and hell are
Now no longer things I fear because
You have saved me
And I'm grateful to the core.
I'm Your child because of Jesus' blood,
And Your Spirit leads me,
Guides me, fills me.

Gareth Robinson
Copyright © 2001 Kingsway's Thankyou Music, P.O. Box 75,
Eastbourne, East Sussex, BN23 6NW, UK. tym@kingsway.co.uk.

Holy, holy, holy is the Lord Almighty,
And we rejoice in You alone,
For You are worthy
And You have given life to me,
And I love to worship at Your feet,
And I love to love You just for who You are.

I'm so grateful for the things
You have given me:
Your love, Your grace, Your joy,
Your peace and more.
Holy, holy.
Holy, holy.

Heaven opened and You came to save me.
You were broken and became sin for me.
No death, no hate, no shame,
No slave again to fear;
New life, new hope, new love,
Your kingdom's coming near.

And I give You praise
And I lift my hands to You,
All of my days
I will bring my love to You.
I will give my life as an offering,
As a sacrifice to the coming King of grace,
Jesus.

You have risen from the grave forever.
Through eternity I'll praise my Saviour.
No death, no hate, no shame,
No slave again to fear;
New life, new hope, new love,
Your kingdom's coming near.

I love and adore You
And live for Your praise.
In truth and in spirit
I long for You, my King.

Ken Riley
Copyright © 2001 Kingsway's Thankyou Music, P.O. Box 75,
Eastbourne, East Sussex, BN23 6NW, UK. tym@kingsway.co.uk

CCL Licence no. _____

Hey, Lord, (Hey, Lord),
O, Lord, (O, Lord),
Hey, Lord, (Hey, Lord),
You know what we need.
(Repeat)

Na na na na na na na,
Na na na na na na na,
Na na na na na na na na.

Jesus, (Jesus),
You're the One (You're the One),
You set my heart (You set my heart)
On fire (on fire).
(Repeat)

Kevin Prosch
Copyright © 1996 Kevin Prosch/Adm. by Kingsway's Thankyou Music,
P.O. Box 75 Eastbourne, East Sussex, BN23 6NW, UK. tym@kingsway.co.uk.
For Europe (excl. Germany, Austria, Switzerland, Liechtenstein and
Luxembourg).

CCL Licence no. _____

Holy, holy, holy, holy
Is the Lord God Almighty.
Holy, holy, holy, holy
Is the song around the throne.
Where the angels and the elders gather
There in sweet assembly,
Singing holy, singing holy
Is the Lord our God.

Worthy, worthy, worthy, worthy
Is the Lamb who was slain for me.
Worthy, worthy, worthy, worthy
Is the song within my heart.
I could choose to spend eternity
With this my sole refrain:
Singing worthy, singing worthy,
Is the Lord our God.

The Way, the Truth,
The Life, the Light,
The King, the Great I Am.
My life, my all,
My every breath,
The Rock on which I stand.

Robin Mark
Copyright © 2000 Kingsway's Thankyou Music, P.O. Box 75, Eastbourne, East
Sussex, BN23 6NW, UK. tym@kingsway.co.uk

Oh Jesus, oh Jesus,
How You suffered and died for us.
Oh Jesus, oh Jesus,
But that tomb is empty now.
And I long to gaze upon Your throne
And all Your risen glory:
Singing Jesus, singing Jesus
Is the Lord of all.

The Way, the Truth,
The Life, the Light,
The King, the Great I Am.
My life, my all,
My every breath,
The Rock on which I stand.

Hope has found its home within me,
Now that I've been found in You.
Let all I am be all You want me to be,
'Cause all I want is more of You,
All I want is more of You.

Let Your presence fall upon us,
I want to see You face to face;
Let me live forever lost in Your love,
'Cause all I want is more of You,
All I want is more of You.

I'm living for this cause,
I lay down my life
Into Your hands.
I'm living for the truth,
The hope of the world,
In You I'll stand.
All I want is You.

All I want is,
All I want is You, Jesus.

Joel Houston
Copyright © 2000 Joel Houston/Hillsong Publishing/Kingsway's
Thankyou Music, P.O. Box 75, Eastbourne, East Sussex, BN23 6NW, UK.
tym@kingsway.co.uk. For UK & Europe.

I am helplessly in love with You.
I am lost in something precious.
I am drowning in the sea of You.
I am found amongst Your treasures.

And I don't know why You give Yourself,
And I can't explain why You should care.
When all heaven sings Your glory,
I'm humbled that You hear my prayer.

I can only give my heart to You,
I can only give my heart.
(Repeat)

I am helplessly devoted to You;
I am scorched by strange new fire.
I am running deeper into You.
I am high upon the wire.

It's like breathing some strange new air,
Walking on some distant moon.
I'll sing a song from the depths of my soul:
Seeking, finding, coming home.
Seeking, finding, coming home.

Sue Rinaldi/Caroline Bonnett/Steve Bassett
Copyright © 2001 Kingsway's Thankyou Music, P.O. Box 75,
Eastbourne, East Sussex, BN23 6NW, UK. tym@kingsway.co.uk.

CCL licence no. _____

I am so tired of compromising.
I am so tired of lukewarm living.
So here I am,
My arms wide open.
Lord, here I am,
My heart wide open.

Set me on fire,
Set me on fire.
Set me on fire,
Set me on fire.

Take this heart of mine,
Place Your love inside.
I want to go against the grain,
I want to go against the grain.

I come to You, to sit at Your feet,
I hear You call, I'm longing to meet You.
I lift my face to You, and catch Your eye,
Oh how You satisfy.

Jesus, Your love surrounds me.
Jesus, Your love completes me.

Now looking closer, I see the scars,
Stories of love, You paid the greatest price,
So that I may have life.
Thank You, my Friend,
You're showing me once again.

There's nothing like it,
There's nothing like it,
There's nothing like the love of God.
(Repeat)

No longer searching, I've found the One,
Just touched the surface, only begun,
This love goes deeper
Than any I've known.

Nathan Fellingham
Copyright © 2001 Kingsway's Thankyou Music, P.O. Box 75,
Eastbourne, East Sussex, BN23 6NW, UK. tym@kingsway.co.uk.

I count as nothing
Every earthly treasure, Jesus:
What You have shown me is that
You are the source of my life.
So what else can I do
But stay here?

Why would I look
For any worldly pleasure, Jesus,
When I have all things in You?
And just a heart beat away.
So what else can I do
But stay here with You?

You're all that I need,
You're all that I need,
So here I'll stay
And give my praise to You.

Neil Bennetts
Copyright © 2001 Kingsway's Thankyou Music, P.O. Box 75,
Eastbourne, East Sussex, BN23 6NW, UK. tym@kingsway.co.uk.

I have come to realise
The glory of the Lord resides
In this jar of clay.
If my world is going to see
The glory of the Lord revealed,
Then my pride must break.
Then the fragrance of Jesus
Will be released,
And the glory of God will be revealed
In all my world.

Jesus, let Your name
Be fragrant in me,
Like perfume that's poured
From this vessel of clay.

And I will live all my days
To be the praise,
And I will live all my days
To be the praise of Your glory.

Andrew Rogers
Copyright © 2001 Kingsway's Thankyou Music, P.O. Box 75,
Eastbourne, East Sussex, BN23 6NW, UK. tym@kingsway.co.uk.

I look into the eyes of love,
And I see joy unending;
My Father's face shines on me.
Your waves of grace come crashing in,
Removing every blot of sin,
And now my heart, it can sing.

Everloving, gracious, Father King
Poured His love on me,
Breaking every chain that held me down.
(Repeat)

And now I stand before the throne,
For I've been counted righteous,
Because of blood shed for me.
Here I will join the massive throng,
As we all sing salvation's song,
The Son of God has set us free!

You are my Lover, Saviour and my Friend,
You hold me close when I cry.
Never leaving, ever present,
Always by my side;
You are my heart's true desire.
(Repeat)

Doug Hawkins
Copyright © 2001 Kingsway's Thankyou Music, P.O. Box 75,
Eastbourne, East Sussex, BN23 6NW, UK. tym@kingsway.co.uk.

CCL licence no. _____

I love You more each day,
With all my heart can give;
Worship at Your feet,
Lost within Your gaze.
Just to know that You're near,
My treasure is here,
And that You gave Your life
To save me.
How my heart sings with praise
And calls on Your name:
My Saviour, my Lover, my King,
Come to me again!

In Christ alone my hope is found,
He is my light, my strength, my song;
This Cornerstone, this solid Ground,
Firm through the fiercest drought and storm.
What heights of love, what depths of peace,
When fears are stilled, when strivings cease!
My Comforter, my All in All,
Here in the love of Christ I stand.

In Christ alone! - who took on flesh,
Fullness of God in helpless babe!
This gift of love and righteousness,
Scorned by the ones He came to save:
Till on that cross as Jesus died,
The wrath of God was satisfied –
For every sin on Him was laid;
Here in the death of Christ I live.

Words: Stuart Townend. Music: Keith Getty
Copyright © 2001 Kingsway's Thankyou Music, P.O. Box 75,
Eastbourne, East Sussex, BN23 6NW, UK. tym@kingsway.co.uk.

CCL licence no. _____

There in the ground His body lay,
Light of the world by darkness slain:
Then bursting forth in glorious Day
Up from the grave He rose again!
And as He stands in victory
Sin's curse has lost its grip on me,
For I am His and He is mine –
Bought with the precious blood of Christ.

No guilt in life, no fear in death,
This is the power of Christ in me;
From life's first cry to final breath,
Jesus commands my destiny.
No power of hell, no scheme of man,
Can ever pluck me from His hand;
Till He returns or calls me home,
Here in the power of Christ I'll stand!

In awe of You, we worship,
And stand amazed at Your great love.
We're changed from glory to glory,
We set our hearts on You, our God.

Now Your presence fills this place,
Be exalted in our praise.
As we worship I believe
You are near.
(Repeat)

Blessing and honour
And glory and power
Forever, forever.
(Repeat)

Reuben Morgan
Copyright © 1999 Reuben Morgan/Hillsong Publishing/Kingsway's
Thankyou Music, P.O. Box 75, Eastbourne, East Sussex, BN23 6NW, UK.
tym@kingsway.co.uk. For the UK & Europe.

CCL licence no. _____

In every day that dawns,
I see the light of Your splendour around me;
And everywhere I turn,
I know the gift of Your favour upon me.
What can I do but give You glory, Lord?
Everything good has come from You.

I'm grateful for the air I breathe,
I'm so thankful for this life I live,
For the mercies that You pour on me,
And the blessings that meet every need.
And the grace that is changing me
From a hopeless case to a child that's free,
Free to give You praise,
For in everything
I know You love me.
I know You love me.

Through all that I have known,
I have been held in the shelter of Your hand;
And as my life unfolds,
You are revealing the wisdom
Of Your sovereign plan.
There are no shadows in Your faithfulness,
There are no limits to Your love.

Kate Simmonds & Stuart Townend
Copyright © 2001 Kingsway's Thankyou Music, P.O. Box 75,
Eastbourne, East Sussex, BN23 6NW, UK. tym@kingsway.co.uk.

All night long on my bed I looked for the one my heart loves; I looked for him but did not find him. I will get up now and go about the city, through the streets and squares; I will search for the one my heart loves.

SONG OF SONGS 3:1-2

In this place we gather
To worship You together,
To come before You, holy God.
(Repeat)

And as we seek Your face,
Let this be Your dwelling place,
We have come to worship You.
We come to give our all,
It's at Your feet we fall,
We have come to praise You.

We have come to worship,
We have come to worship,
We have come to worship You.

I see You hanging there,
Nailed to a splintered wooden beam,
Drinking pain and sorrows,
Breathing agony.
And in those dark, dark hours,
As life drained from Your flesh and bones,
I know my life had its beginning
At Your cross.
And I thank You, thank You:

For the cross, where You bled,
For the cross, where You died,
For the cross,
Where You've broken Satan's back.
For the cross, where You won,
For the cross of victory,
For the cross,
Where You paid the price for me.

You were my substitute
In laying down Your life for mine,
Being cursed and bearing
The wrath of God for me.
You were crushed by sin,
Your punishment has brought me peace,
And by the wounds You suffered
I'm alive and healed.
And I thank You, thank You.

Two days in the grave,
Then You rose up from the dead –
Now You reign in glory,
Rule in righteousness.
And I was raised with You,
Free at last from all my sin,
Safe forever in the shelter of my King.
And I thank You, thank You.

For the cross, where You bled,
For the cross where You died,
For the cross,
Where You've broken Satan's back.
For the cross, where You won,
For the cross of victory,
For the cross,
Where You paid the price for me.

I've filled my days with details
And all the choices of the earth,
Carried the yoke of worry,
And all the burdens that it brings.
So through the midst of all the rushing,
You whisper to our hearts,
And with Your sweet voice
You say to us:

To be still and know You are God,
To be still and know You are God,
Just to rest in Your arms.

So give me peace and wisdom
To know how to fill my time,
Where I can learn to keep You
At the centre of my life.
So through the midst of all the rushing
There is time to spend with You,
And my foundation
Will daily be:

David Gate
Copyright © 2001 Kingsway's Thankyou Music, P.O. Box 75,
Eastbourne, East Sussex, BN23 6NW, UK. tym@kingsway.co.uk.

CCL Licence no. _____

I will come, come, come
To the waters and drink,
I will praise, praise, praise Your name again.
I will rest, rest, rest, rest at Your feet,
For You have won my heart once again.

I will thirst, thirst, thirst for all that You give,
I will fall, fall, fall into Your arms again.
I will call, call, call to You alone each day,
For You have won my heart once again.

And You are God with fire in Your eyes,
You are God adorned in radiant light.
You are God
Whose hands were pierced for all:
What choice do I have
But to give You my very all?

I shall wait, wait, wait
At the cross where we meet,
And I will live, live, live
By Your name I speak.
I will run, run, run for Your face to seek,
For You have won my heart once again.

Tim Sherrington
Copyright © 2000 Kingsway's Thankyou Music, P.O. Box 75,
Eastbourne, East Sussex, BN23 6NW, UK. tym@kingsway.co.uk.

CCL licence no. _____

Jesus, all for Jesus;
All I am and have and ever hope to be.
Jesus, all for Jesus;
All I am and have and ever hope to be.
For it's only in Your will that I am free.
For it's only in Your will that I am free.
Jesus, all for Jesus;
All I am and have and ever hope to be.

All of my ambitions, hopes and plans,
I surrender these into Your hands.
All of my ambitions, hopes and plans,
I surrender these into Your hands.
For it's only in Your will that I am free.
For it's only in Your will that I am free.
Jesus, all for Jesus;
All I am and have and ever hope to be.

Jennifer Atkinson & Robin Mark
Copyright © 1991 Word's Spirit of Praise Music/Adm. by CopyCare,
P.O. Box 77, Hailsham, East Sussex, BN27 3EF, UK. music@copycare.com.

CCL Licence no. _____

Jesus, Jesus, Jesus,
How I love Your name.

The sweetest song on earth
Will never be enough
To tell the wonder of Your love.
Come hide me in Your arms,
And calm my restless heart;
I hunger, Lord, for more of You.

Dave Bilbrough
Copyright © 2000 Kingsway's Thankyou Music, P.O. Box 75,
Eastbourne, East Sussex, BN23 6NW, UK. tym@kingsway.co.uk.

CCL Licence no. _____

Jesus, Name above all names,
My soul cries Jesus,
It's the sweetest song.
Jesus, echoing throughout
All of the heavens,
Angelic hosts proclaim.

Morning Star, Rising Sun,
Lily of the valley,
Rose of Sharon, Son of God.
Lifted up, glorified,
Praised through all the ages;
The First and Last, Beginning and End.

Owen Hurter
Copyright © 2000 Kingsway's Thankyou Music, P.O. Box 75,
Eastbourne, East Sussex, BN23 6NW, UK. tym@kingsway.co.uk.

CCL Licence no. _____

Jesus, Redeemer,
Friend and King to me.
My refuge, my comfort,
You're everything to me.

And this heart is on fire for You,
Yes, this heart is on fire for You.

For You alone are wonderful,
You alone are Counsellor,
Everlasting Father, mighty in the heavens.
Never to forget the love
You displayed upon a cross.
Son of God I thank You;
Prince of Peace, I love Your name.

Saviour, Healer,
Just and true are You.
Now reigning in glory,
Most high and living God.

And this heart is in awe of You,
Yes, this heart is in awe of You.

Tim Hughes
Copyright © 2001 Kingsway's Thankyou Music, P.O. Box 75,
Eastbourne, East Sussex, BN23 6NW, UK. tym@kingsway.co.uk.

Jesus taught us how to pray:
Father hallowed be Your name.
Would You give us what we need,
And forgive our foolish ways?

I know Jesus only prayed,
Father, what You had ordained.

Let Your kingdom come on earth Lord,
As we pray.
Let Your will be done to glorify Your name.
Let the kingdom that we live for
Be revealed in us today.
Can I see heaven, can I see heaven
Here on earth today?

Knowing Your grace
Has set me free, Lord.
I'm seeking Your face;
I feel Your pleasure,
Your joy in the ones
You have chosen by name.
You've lifted my burdens
And cast off my shame.

Feeling Your touch
Gives me such peace, Lord.
I love You so much,
I know You'll lead me.
Wherever I go I'll be under Your wing,
For I am a child of the King.

You will finish the work You've begun in me,
I'm adopted, a son in Your family!
You've drawn me with kindness and love
Into this holy place.

What can I say?
Your lavish mercy
Turned night into day –
My guilt has gone now.
Forever I'll stand in Your presence and sing,
For I am a child of the King.

Terry Virgo & Stuart Townend
Copyright © 2001 Kingsway's Thankyou Music, P.O. Box 75,
Eastbourne, East Sussex, BN23 6NW, UK. tym@kingsway.co.uk.

Light of the world,
You stepped down into darkness,
Opened my eyes, let me see
Beauty that made this heart adore You,
Hope of a life spent with You.

So here I am to worship,
Here I am to bow down,
Here I am to say that You're my God.
And You're altogether lovely,
Altogether worthy,
Altogether wonderful to me.

King of all days, oh so highly exalted,
Glorious in heaven above.
Humbly You came to the earth You created,
All for love's sake became poor.

And I'll never know how much it cost
To see my sin upon that cross.
(Repeat)

Tim Hughes
Copyright © 2001 Kingsway's Thankyou Music, P.O. Box 75,
Eastbourne, East Sussex, BN23 6NW, UK. tym@kingsway.co.uk.

CCL Licence no. _____

Like a fragrant oil,
Like costly perfume poured forth,
Let my worship be to You.
Like a fervent prayer,
Like incense rising to Your throne,
In spirit and in truth.

Jesus,
You alone are worthy of my praise,
I owe my life to You.
Jesus,
You alone can make me holy,
So I bow before You.

Like a wedding vow,
'All I am I give to You,'
Let my sacrifice be pure.
Like the sweetest sound,
Like a lover's whisper in Your ear,
I've set my heart on You.

Look what You've done in my life,
See what You've done in this heart;
You've brought hope, healing and freedom,
Look what You've done in my life.
(Repeat)

And though I'm not deserving of Your love,
You give it all to me,
With open arms You welcome me.

Your love is higher than the mountains,
Your love is deeper than the sea.
Jesus, You came to pay my ransom,
It's Your love, Jesus, that sets me free.

Eoghan Heaslip & M. Goss
Copyright © 1999 Daybreak Music, Silverdale Road,
Eastbourne, East Sussex, BN20 7AB, UK.

Lord, You are my righteousness,
The One who sanctifies my life,
My Shepherd and my guide.
Banner of deliverance,
Warrior and my defence,
In Your secret place I hide.
Every other throne must fall
And proclaim You Lord of all
At the mention of Your name;
My salvation and my light,
In Your presence I abide
And Your righteousness I claim.

Jesus, Jesus,
Jesus, Jesus.

Though You are the King of kings,
Yet You are my next of kin,
And my nearest friend.
Laying down Your life for me,
Your amazing grace I see,
And Your love without an end.
How can I keep silent, Lord?
Even stones obey Your word
And they give to You their praise.
You're the Lord of everything,
All creation's voices sing
Of the glory of Your name.

May the words of my mouth,
And the thoughts of my heart
Bless Your name, bless Your name, Jesus.
And the deeds of the day,
And the truth in my ways,
Speak of You, speak of You, Jesus.

For this is what I'm glad to do,
It's time to live a life of love
That pleases You.
And I will give my all to You,
Surrender everything I have and follow You,
I'll follow You.

Lord, will You be my vision,
Lord, will You be my guide?
Be my hope, be my light, and the way.
And I'll look not for riches,
Nor praises on earth,
Only You'll be the first of my heart.

I will follow, I will follow,
I will follow You.
(Repeat x4)

Tim Hughes & Rob Hill
Copyright © 2000 Kingsway's Thankyou Music, P.O. Box 75,
Eastbourne, East Sussex, BN23 6NW, UK. tym@kingsway.co.uk.

CCL licence no. _____

More than I could hope or dream of,
You have poured Your favour on me.
One day in the house of God
Is better than a thousand days in the world.

So blessed, I can't contain it,
So much, I've got to give it away.
Your love has taught me how to live now,
You are more than enough for me.

Lord, You're more than enough for me,
More than enough for me.

Reuben Morgan
Copyright © 1999 Reuben Morgan/Hillsong Publishing/Kingsway's
Thankyou Music, P.O. Box 75, Eastbourne, East Sussex, BN23 6NW, UK.
tym@kingsway.co.uk. For the UK & Europe.

CCL licence no. _____

My hope is in the Lord,
Who has renewed my strength;
When everything seems senseless,
My hope is still in Him.
Who has made heaven and earth
And things seen and unseen,
Whatever shade of passing day,
My hope is still in Him.

My hope is in You, Lord.
My hope is in You, Lord.
My hope is in You, Lord.
My hope is in You, Lord.

For I know that my eyes shall see You
In the latter days to come.
When You stand on the earth,
With my lips I will confess
That the hope of my heart is come,
That the hope of my heart is come.

Robin Mark
Copyright © 2000 Kingsway's Thankyou Music, P.O. Box 75,
Eastbourne, East Sussex, BN23 6NW, UK. tym@kingsway.co.uk.

CCL licence no. _____

My hope rests firm on Jesus Christ,
He is my only plea:
Though all the world should point and
    scorn,
His ransom leaves me free,
His ransom leaves me free.

My hope sustains me as I strive
And strain towards the goal;
Though still I stumble into sin,
His death paid for it all,
His death paid for it all.

My hope provides me with a spur
To help me run this race:
I know my tears will turn to joy
The day I see His face,
The day I see His face.

My hope is to be with my Lord,
To know as I am known:
To serve Him gladly all my days
In praise before His throne,
In praise before His throne.

Richard Creighton & Keith Getty
Copyright © 2001 Kingsway's Thankyou Music, P.O. Box 75,
Eastbourne, East Sussex, BN23 6NW, UK. tym@kingsway.co.uk.

CCL licence no. _____

Name above all names,
The Saviour for sinners slain.
You suffered for my sake
To bring me back home again.
When I was lost,
You poured Your life out for me.
Name above all names,
Jesus, I love You.

Giver of mercy,
The fountain of life for me.
My spirit is lifted,
To soar on the eagle's wings.
What love is this
That fills my heart with treasure?
Name above all names,
Jesus, I love You.

High King eternal,
The one true and faithful God.
The beautiful Saviour,
Still reigning in power and love.
With all my heart
I'll worship You forever:
Name above all names,
Jesus, I love You.

Neil Bennetts
Copyright © 2000 Daybreak Music Ltd, Silverdale Road,
Eastbourne, East Sussex, BN20 7AB, UK.

Nothing is too much to ask,
Now that I have said I'm Yours.
Jesus take the whole of me,
Unreservedly.

Jesus take me deeper now,
That I might go further too.
I've received so much from You,
Undeservedly.

I was made to love You, Lord,
I was saved to worship You.
You will be the focus of
All eternity.

Matt Redman & Mike Pilavachi
Copyright © 2000 Kingsway's Thankyou Music, P.O. Box 75,
Eastbourne, East Sussex, BN23 6NW, UK. tym@kingsway.co.uk.

CCL licence no. _____

Oh fallen one, covered now in shame,
He is your hope, He is your life.
Though He should judge,
His anger turns away;
Rise from the dust, beautiful one.

Don't be afraid,
For you're not left alone;
His heart of love is broken for you.
Your Father cares
For all your children now,
Arise in His name, beautiful one.

Arise and shine, your glory has come,
Arise and shine, your glory has come,
Arise and shine,
He is calling you by name;
Though your walls have fallen down,
He'll build you up again.

James Gregory
Copyright © 2000 Kingsway's Thankyou Music, P.O. Box 75,
Eastbourne, East Sussex, BN23 6NW, UK. tym@kingsway.co.uk.

CCL licence no. _____

Lift up your eyes,
Many come to see
The splendour your God has given to you.
Could each of your saints
Become a thousand saints?
Rise up and praise, beautiful one.

Arise and shine, your glory has come,
Arise and shine, your glory has come,
Arise and shine,
He is calling you by name;
Though your walls have fallen down,
He'll build you up again.

So let Your salvation come,
For Your glory, Lord.
Set the captives free we pray;
These souls are Your reward.

O Lord, when I wake up in the morning,
Let my mouth be filled with praise for You.
O Lord, when I go out in the evening,
Let my mouth be filled with praise for You.
That all might know and many might see,
That You're my Lord.

Fill me with a spirit of boldness,
Oh my God,
And come and take all of my shame;
That I might see temptation
Melt before my eyes
And watch the demons flee in Jesus' name,
As we lift high the name.

Lift high the name of the Lord.
Lift high the name of the Lord.
That many might know,
That many might see my Lord.

Brian Houston
Copyright © 2000 Kingsway's Thankyou Music, P.O. Box 75,
Eastbourne, East Sussex, BN23 6NW, UK. tym@kingsway.co.uk.

CCL licence no. _____

O Lord, when I'm stressed and feeling tired,
Let my mouth be filled with praise to You.
O Lord, when I'm pressed on every side,
Let my mouth be filled with praise to You,
That all might know and many might see
That You are Lord.

Fill me with a spirit of boldness,
Oh my God,
And come and take all of my shame;
That I might see temptation
Melt before my eyes
And watch the demons flee in Jesus' name,
As we lift high the name.

Lift high the name of the Lord.
Lift high the name of the Lord.
That many might know,
That many might see my Lord.

Only You can replace
Rags for riches pure as gold,
And Your mercy saved my soul,
There's none like You.

At Your name demons flee,
Mountains tremble in Your sight,
But You love me like a friend,
There's none like You.

Nothing compares to You,
You're the One we love.
Send down Your holy fire
Over all the earth.
Nothing compares to You,
You're the One we love.

You have paid such a cost,
So much more than can be won:
God, You gave Your only Son,
There's none like You.

So we'll bow to the cross
Where the tears of heaven fall.
You have heard the sinner's call:
There's none like You.

James Taylor
Copyright © 2000 Kingsway's Thankyou Music, P.O. Box 75,
Eastbourne, East Sussex, BN23 6NW, UK. tym@kingsway.co.uk.

CCL licence no. _____

Open the eyes of my heart, Lord,
Open the eyes of my heart.
I want to see You,
I want to see You.
(Repeat)

To see You high and lifted up,
Shining in the light of Your glory.
Pour out Your power and love,
As we sing holy, holy, holy.

Holy, holy, holy,
Holy, holy, holy,
Holy, holy, holy,
I want to see You.

Salvation spring up from the ground,
Lord, rend the heavens and come down.
Seek the lost and heal the lame;
Jesus, bring glory to Your name.
Let all the prodigals run home,
All of creation waits and groans.
Lord, we've heard of Your great fame;
Father, cause all to shout Your name.

Stir up our hearts, O God;
Open our spirits to awe who You are.
Put a cry in us
So deep inside,
That we cannot find
The words we need,
We just weep and cry out to You.

Sing praises to our God, sing praises.
Sing praises to the King, sing praises.
(Repeat)

For God is King of all the earth,
Sing to Him a psalm of praise.
God reigns over the nations,
All our worship we will raise.
He's King of all the earth,
Bring to Him a joyful song.
He's Lord of all creation,
Seated on His holy throne.

Clap your hands, all you nations,
Shout to God with cries of joy,
How awesome is the Lord most high.
Clap your hands, all creation,
Cry to God who made us all,
The great King over all the world.

David Lyle Morris
Copyright © 2001 Kingsway's Thankyou Music, P.O. Box 75,
Eastbourne, East Sussex, BN23 6NW, UK. tym@kingsway.co.uk.

CCL licence no. _____

Spirit move on this land,
Take Your people in Your hands.
We're waiting for the day,
The day You come again.
Your Spirit is coming to give to the poor;
So Father, take our lives and shine.

Revival in our land,
Won't rest until we see
Revival in our land.
Revival in our land,
Won't rest until we see
Revival in our land.

Tim Sherrington
Copyright © 2001 Kingsway's Thankyou Music, P.O. Box 75,
Eastbourne, East Sussex, BN23 6NW, UK. tym@kingsway.co.uk.

CCL licence no. _____

Standing on holy ground,
Mercy and grace I've found.
I'm here before Your throne now,
By a new and living way.
Jesus, I come to You.
I lift up my eyes to You.
How You've comforted me,
And now I long to see Your face.

You are my strength, my song;
You are my shield, my Redeemer.
You are my hope, my salvation,
And my God.
I'll always bring my praise to You,
O God.
(2nd time)
So I will sing to You,
Beautiful things You have done.
Great is Your name in Zion,
Holy One.
I'll always bring my praise to You,
I'll always bring my praise to You,
I'll always bring my praise to You,
O God.

Paul Oakley & Martin Cooper
Copyright © 2001 Kingsway's Thankyou Music, P.O. Box 75,
Eastbourne, East Sussex, BN23 6NW, UK. tym@kingsway.co.uk.

CCL licence no. _____

Teach me of Your ways,
To honour You with all I have,
And that I learn to say:
"Not my will, but Yours, my Lord."

O Jesus, be glorified
With all of my life.
It's all about You,
And the worship You're due.
So help me to change,
Mould me like clay;
Lord, have Your way,
Lord, have Your way with me.

Lord I long to be
A faithful child who honours You.
So Jesus be in me,
Let Your light shine through me now.

David Gate
Copyright © 2001 Kingsway's Thankyou Music, P.O. Box 75,
Eastbourne, East Sussex, BN23 6NW, UK. tym@kingsway.co.uk.

CCL licence no. _____

The place where You dwell
Is where I want to be,
It's where angels in splendour
Worship the King.
And to Jesus in glory
Each voice raised in song:
Holy, holy, holy is the Lord.

In the light of Your presence
I find perfect peace,
And my heart shall adore You
And in You rejoice.
And to Jesus victorious
I lift up my song:
Worthy, worthy, worthy is the Lamb.

It's all for You, Jesus,
Only You, Jesus.
You are my song and my reason to sing,
You have set this heart free
To rise on the wings of Your praise.

Ed Pask
Copyright © 2001 Kingsway's Thankyou Music, P.O. Box 75,
Eastbourne, East Sussex, BN23 6NW, UK. tym@kingsway.co.uk.

There is a day
That all creation's waiting for,
A day of freedom and liberation for the
    earth.
And on that day
The Lord will come to meet His bride,
And when we see Him
In an instant we'll be changed.

The trumpet sounds
And the dead will then be raised
By His power,
Never to perish again.
Once only flesh,
Now clothed with immortality;
Death has now been
Swallowed up in victory.

We will meet Him in the air
And then we will be like Him,
For we will see Him, as He is,
Oh yeah!
Then all hurt and pain will cease,
And we'll be with Him forever,
And in His glory we will live,
Oh yeah, oh yeah!

Nathan Fellingham
Copyright © 2001 Kingsway's Thankyou Music, P.O. Box 75,
Eastbourne, East Sussex, BN23 6NW, UK. tym@kingsway.co.uk.

CCL licence no. _____

So lift your eyes
To the things as yet unseen,
That will remain now
For all eternity.
Though trouble's hard
It's only momentary,
And it's achieving
Our future glory.

We will meet Him in the air
And then we will be like Him,
For we will see Him, as He is,
Oh yeah!
Then all hurt and pain will cease,
And we'll be with Him forever,
And in His glory we will live,
Oh yeah, oh yeah!

You also, like living stones, are being built into a spiritual house to be a holy priesthood, offering spiritual sacrifices acceptable to God through Jesus Christ.

1 PETER 2:5

There is a name that's high over all.
There is a King seated on the throne.
And He's interceding for me,
So that I will be made holy,
And I know that in His love
I will stay.

What a Saviour is my Jesus,
He came down
So that I may go free.

There is a Man who walked on the earth,
The Word of God made known to us.
He's the image of the Father,
The Firstborn over creation,
Yet He suffered at the hands of those He
     saves.

What a Saviour is my Jesus,
He came down
So that I may go free.
How I love You, oh my Jesus,
You came down
So that I may go free.

Nathan Fellingham
Copyright © 2001 Kingsway's Thankyou Music, P.O. Box 75,
Eastbourne, East Sussex, BN23 6NW, UK. tym@kingsway.co.uk.

CCL licence no. _____

There's a call to the people of Zion,
To arise and possess the land;
Every town has its heirs to the promise,
Every nation its sons of light.
We have stayed long enough on this
    mountain,
Now we're called to new realms of faith;
We are more than a temple of worship,
We're an army of praise!

We will go to every place,
Sharing mercy and preaching grace,
For the fields are white for harvest,
And labourers are few.
No place too dark, no soul too lost
For the power of the cross;
For His light will shine in darkness,
And many will believe,
So we will go.

Stuart Townend
Copyright © 2001 Kingsway's Thankyou Music, P.O. Box 75,
Eastbourne, East Sussex, BN23 6NW, UK. tym@kingsway.co.uk.

CCL licence no. _____

We have drunk of the wine of His presence,
We have feasted upon His word;
Now we're hungry for works of power,
Now we're thirsty to share His love.
He will give us the ground that we walk on,
For the battle belongs to God;
Do not fear, for His grace is sufficient,
When we're weak, He is strong!

We will go to every place,
Sharing mercy and preaching grace,
For the fields are white for harvest,
And labourers are few.
No place too dark, no soul too lost
For the power of the cross;
For His light will shine in darkness,
And many will believe,
So we will go.

We fall down,
We lay our crowns
At the feet of Jesus.
The greatness of mercy and love,
At the feet of Jesus.

And we cry holy, holy, holy.
And we cry holy, holy, holy.
And we cry holy, holy, holy
Is the Lamb.

Chris Tomlin
Copyright © 1998 worshiptogether.com songs/EMI Christian Music Publishing/
Adm. by CopyCare, P.O. Box 77, Hailsham, East Sussex, BN27 3EF, UK.
music@copycare.com.

CCL licence no. _____

We're gonna sing like the saved,
We're gonna sing like the saved,
We're gonna sing like the saved,
We're gonna sing like the saved.

It is our duty and our joy,
In every time and every place,
Your gates we'll enter to give thanks,
Your courts we'll run into with praise.

A joyful noise we will make...

You put Your joy in our hearts...

We're gonna dance like the saved...

Matt Redman
Copyright © 1998 Kingsway's Thankyou Music, P.O. Box 75,
Eastbourne, East Sussex, BN23 6NW, UK. tym@kingsway.co.uk.

We've come to praise You,
'Cause You're worthy.
Nobody like You in Your glory.
We love to praise You,
'Cause You're holy, awesome,
Wonderful, mighty God.

And everything that You do
Comes from a heart of love
And a hand of mercy;
For You are faithful and true,
Working all things for good
For those who love You.

For if God in love did not spare His Son,
But He gave Him up for His chosen ones,
How much more will He freely give to us
Who call upon His name? (x4)

What to say, Lord?
It's You who gave me life,
And I can't explain
Just how much You mean to me now
That You have saved me, Lord.
I give all that I am to You,
That every day I can be a light
That shines Your name.

Every day, Lord,
I'll learn to stand upon Your word,
And pray that I,
That I might come to know You more;
That You would guide me
In every single step I take,
That every day I can be
Your light unto the world.

Every day, it's You I'll live for,
Every day, I'll follow after You.
Every day, I'll walk with You, my Lord.
(Repeat)

It's You I live for every day. (x6)

What can I say, but 'I love You'?
What can I say, but 'I praise You'?
As the train of Your robe fills this temple,
As the sound of Your voice fills this place.

What can I do, but to bow down?
What can I do, but to worship?
Only You are the One who is worthy,
Only You are the One who is Lord.

Great is the Lord, so great is the Lord,
Righteous and true God, holy and pure.
I fall on my knees confessing my need
For more of Your presence, Lord.

Neil Bennetts
Copyright © 2001 Kingsway's Thankyou Music, P.O. Box 75,
Eastbourne, East Sussex, BN23 6NW, UK. tym@kingsway.co.uk.

CCL licence no. _____

When I survey the wondrous cross
On which the Prince of Glory died,
My richest gain I count but loss,
And pour contempt on all my pride.

See from His head, His hands, His feet,
Sorrow and love flow mingled down;
Did e'er such love and sorrow meet
Or thorns compose so rich a crown?

Oh, the wonderful cross,
Oh, the wonderful cross
Bids me come and die and find
That I may truly live.
Oh, the wonderful cross,
Oh, the wonderful cross,
All who gather here by grace
Draw near and bless Your name.

Were the whole realm of nature mine,
That were an offering far too small.
Love so amazing, so divine
Demands my soul, my life, my all.

Isaac Watts (1674-1748)
Refrain Chris Tomlin & J.D. Walt
Copyright © 2000 worshiptogether.com songs/Six Steps Music/
EMI Christian Music Publishing/Adm. by CopyCare, P.O. Box 77,
Hailsham, East Sussex, BN27 3EF, UK. music@copycare.com.

CCL licence no. _____

When Love came down to earth
And made His home with men,
The hopeless found a hope,
The sinner found a friend.
Not to the powerful
But to the poor He came,
And humble, hungry hearts
Were satisfied again.

What joy, what peace has come to us!
What hope, what help, what love!

When every unclean thought,
And every sinful deed
Was scourged upon His back
And hammered through His feet.
The Innocent is cursed,
The guilty are released;
The punishment of God
On God has bought me peace.

Stuart Townend
Copyright © 2001 Kingsway's Thankyou Music, P.O. Box 75,
Eastbourne, East Sussex, BN23 6NW, UK. tym@kingsway.co.uk.

Come lay your heavy load
Down at the Master's feet;
Your shame will be removed,
Your joy will be complete.
Come crucify your pride,
And enter as a child;
For those who bow down low
He'll lift up to His side.

What joy, what peace has come to us!
What hope, what help, what love!

When I was lost, You came and rescued me;
Reached down into the pit and lifted me,
O Lord, such love,
I was as far from You as I could be.
You know all the things I've ever done,
But Jesus' blood has cancelled every one.
O Lord, such grace
To qualify me as Your own.

There is a new song in my mouth,
There is a deep cry in my heart,
A hymn of praise to Almighty God -
Hallelujah!
And now I stand firm on this Rock,
My life is hidden now with Christ in God.
The old has gone and the new has come -
Hallelujah!
Your love has lifted me.

Kate & Miles Simmonds
Copyright © 2001 Kingsway's Thankyou Music, P.O. Box 75,
Eastbourne, East Sussex, BN23 6NW, UK. tym@kingsway.co.uk.

CCL licence no. _____

Now I have come into Your family,
For the Son of God has died for me.
O Lord, such peace,
I am as loved by You as I could be.
In the full assurance of Your love,
Now with every confidence we come.
O Lord, such joy
To know that You delight in us.

There is a new song in my mouth,
There is a deep cry in my heart,
A hymn of praise to Almighty God -
Hallelujah!
And now I stand firm on this Rock,
My life is hidden now with Christ in God.
The old has gone and the new has come -
Hallelujah!
Your love has lifted me.

Many are the wonders You have done,
And many are the things that You have
    planned.
How beautiful the grace that gives to us
All that we don't deserve,
All that we cannot earn,
But is a gift of love -
Your love has lifted me.

When we turn our hearts to heaven
And bow down,
We'll see fathers and the children
Reconciled.
We'll be the dreamers of Your dreams.
We'll be the dreamers of Your dreams.

When Your fire falls from heaven,
We will rend our hearts to You,
We will tell it to our children,
All the wonders You have done.
And in every generation
We will sing of Your great love.
When Your fire falls from heaven
We'll return to You again!
We'll be the dreamers of Your dreams.
We'll be the dreamers of Your dreams.

Noel Richards & Ken Riley
Copyright © 2001 Kingsway's Thankyou Music, P.O. Box 75,
Eastbourne, East Sussex, BN23 6NW, UK. tym@kingsway.co.uk.

CCL licence no. _____

Who can compare with You, my Father;
Loving and kind, faithful and true?
When You forgive my heart that is broken,
I gratefully sing my love to You.

I worship You,
I love You:
All that I am sings this song of praise.

Here I will dwell in the arms of my Father,
Knowing Your grace, hearing Your voice.
Trusting Your word, feeling Your peace,
Resting in You and in Your love.

And I abide in You,
I abide with You.

Gareth Robinson
Copyright © 2001 Kingsway's Thankyou Music, P.O. Box 75,
Eastbourne, East Sussex, BN23 6NW, UK. tym@kingsway.co.uk.

CCL licence no. _____

Who's the only light that shines and never
    fades?
The Light of the world, Jesus.
Who's the only light that drives the dark
    away?
The Light of the world, Jesus.

It's all about Jesus, Jesus,
It's all about Jesus, Jesus.

Who's the only Word that made all things?
The Word was God, Jesus.
He's the only truth, the fullness of the Lord,
The Son of God, Jesus.

You're the Way, the Truth and the Life.
You're the Way, the Truth and the Life.

Scott Underwood
Copyright © 1999 Mercy/Vineyard Publishing/Adm. by CopyCare,
P.O. Box 77, Hailsham, East Sussex, BN27 3EF, UK. music@copycare.com.

CCL licence no. _____

Worship the Lord,
See the splendour of His holiness.
Give to the Lord all the glory due His name.
Come and adore,
Come and lay Your hearts before Him.
With thankfulness and love,
Come and shout aloud Your praise.

Declare His glory among all the nations.
Declare His majesty,
His splendour and power.
Proclaim salvation,
His goodness and mercy;
For great is the Lord and most worthy,
Worthy of praise.

We are His people, belonging to our Father,
Set apart for truth, we are chosen by God.
With confidence we come,
We are free and we're forgiven.
Blessed are the ones
Who put their hope in God.

Louise Fellingham
Copyright © 1999 Kingsway's Thankyou Music, PO Box 75,
Eastbourne, East Sussex, BN23 6NW, UK. tym@kingsway.co.uk.

CCL licence no. _____

Please come upon us now,
We want to see Your face, Lord.
Soften our hearts, take us deeper into You.
Spirit, fill our minds
With the knowledge of Your wisdom.
Come and touch our mouths,
Help us tell of all You've done.

Declare His glory among all the nations.
Declare His majesty,
His splendour and power.
Proclaim salvation,
His goodness and mercy,
For great is the Lord and most worthy,
Worthy of praise.

You are all I want,
You're all I need to be set free.
Your cross of death gives life to me,
Your sacrifice brings liberty.
No one else could take my place but You,
The Perfect One, the Holy God,
Revealed as man in Jesus Christ.
Only You could take my sin, so…

I love You, yeah, I love You, Jesus.
I love You, yeah, I love You, Jesus.

I will give to You my everything,
Abandon all my selfish dreams
To live for You and do Your will every day.
You have touched my heart
And made me whole,
You've made me clean, so I will give
My offering of love to You.
All my life lived just for You, 'cause…

Gareth Robinson
Copyright © 2001 Kingsway's Thankyou Music, P.O. Box 75,
Eastbourne, East Sussex, BN23 6NW, UK. tym@kingsway.co.uk.

CCL licence no. _____

You are my anchor,
My light and my salvation.
You are my refuge,
My heart will not fear.
Though my foes surround me on every
 hand,
They will stumble and fall
While in grace I stand.
In my day of trouble
You hide me and set me above
To sing this song of love.

One thing I will ask of You, this will I pray:
To dwell in Your house, O Lord, every day,
To gaze upon Your lovely face
And rest in the Father's embrace.

Teach me Your way, Lord,
Make straight the path before me.
Do not forsake me, my hope is in You.
As I walk through life, I am confident
I will see Your goodness with every step,
And my heart directs me to seek You
In all that I do,
So I will wait for You.

You are the One I love,
You are the One that I adore.
(Repeat)

For You've called me by name,
Drawn me close to Your heart,
Washed away all my shame with Your tears.
For the rest of my days,
I will offer my life
In thanksgiving and praise to my King.

Now with You I will stay,
For Your word is my light,
And Your peace can allay all my fears;
And my victory song
Is the song of the cross,
You have won me love so divine.

Such precious, precious love.

Sue Rinaldi & Caroline Bonnett
Copyright © 2001 Kingsway's Thankyou Music, PO Box 75,
Eastbourne, East Sussex, BN23 6NW, UK. tym@kingsway.co.uk.

CCL licence no. _____

You call us first to love Your name,
To worship You.
To please Your heart our one desire,
O Lord.

If there's one thing we are called to do,
It's to love You, to adore You.
We will bring our all and worship You,
Bow before You, as we love You.

Your honour, Lord, Your name's renown
We long to see.
So let the glory of Your name
Be praised.

I will celebrate this love,
Jesus, You are everything to me.
For what more, Lord, can I do?
I will give this heart, this life to You.

Tim Hughes
Copyright © 2001 Kingsway's Thankyou Music, PO Box 75,
Eastbourne, East Sussex, BN23 6NW, UK. tym@kingsway.co.uk.

CCL licence no. _____

You can have my whole life,
You can come and have it all:
I don't want to go my own way now.
I love to feel Your presence
And I know Your saving grace,
I am nothing when You're second place.

I've been born to give You praise,
Not to yearn and strive for worldly things.
I've been born to love Your ways,
Take my pride and let me always say:
I want to go Your way now.

James Taylor
Copyright © 2001 Kingsway's Thankyou Music, PO Box 75,
Eastbourne, East Sussex, BN23 6NW, UK. tym@kingsway.co.uk.

You pour out grace on the broken-hearted,
And You lift the hope of the weary soul,
And You stretch out Your hand
With Your loving mercy.
You saw this heart that was lost and broken,
And You felt the pain of my loneliness,
And You befriended me
And restored my dignity.

You alone revealed the love of God to me,
And You alone have given everything for me;
And You alone deserve the highest praise,
Jesus.
And You have given me great salvation,
And You have given me hope eternal,
And every day I will look to give You
All the glory that's due Your name.

Gareth Robinson
Copyright © 2001 Kingsway's Thankyou Music, PO Box 75,
Eastbourne, East Sussex, BN23 6NW, UK. tym@kingsway.co.uk.

CCL licence no. _____

Your face outshines the brightest sun,
Jesus, You're glorious,
You are so glorious.
With eyes that blaze like burning fire,
Jesus, You're glorious,
You are so glorious.

King of glory, have Your glory,
King of glory, have Your glory.

Your voice like rushing waters sounds,
Jesus, You're powerful,
You are so powerful.
And in Your hands You hold the stars,
Jesus, You're powerful,
You are so powerful.

Matt Redman & David Gate
Copyright © 2001 Kingsway's Thankyou Music, P.O. Box 75,
Eastbourne, East Sussex, BN23 6NW, UK. tym@kingsway.co.uk.

CCL licence no. _____

Your hand, O God, has guided
Your church from age to age,
The tale of love is written
For us on every page.
Our fathers knew Your goodness,
And we Your works record,
And each of these bear witness:
One church, one faith, one Lord.

One church, one faith, one Lord of life,
One Father, one Spirit, one Christ.
One church, one faith, one Lord of Life,
One heavenly King, Lord of all.

Your mercy never fails us,
Or leaves Your work undone;
With Your right hand to help us,
The victory shall be won.
And then with heaven's angels
Your name shall be adored,
And they shall praise You, singing:
One church, one faith, one Lord.

Words: E.H. Plumptre (1821-91), adpt. Keith Getty.
Copyright © 2001 Kingsway's Thankyou Music, P.O. Box 75,
Eastbourne, East Sussex, BN23 6NW, UK. tym@kingsway.co.uk.

CCL licence no. _____

Your kingdom generation
Declares Your majesty,
And our lives are resounding with Your
     praise.

We see Your Spirit moving,
We burn with holy fire.
Your glory is seen through all the earth.

You set eternity in my heart,
So I'll live for You,
For You.

Hallelujah, hallelujah,
Honour and praise forever.
We'll shout a victory cry
From here to eternity.
Hallelujah, hallelujah,
We'll take our place in history.
We'll shout Your awesome love
From here to eternity.

Darlene Zschech & David Moyse
Copyright © 2000 Darlene Zschech & David Moyse/Hillsong Publishing/
Kingsway's Thankyou Music, P.O. Box 75, Eastbourne, East Sussex,
BN23 6NW, UK. tym@kingsway.co.uk. For the UK & Europe.

CCL licence no. _____

Your love is amazing,
Steady and unchanging;
Your love is a mountain,
Firm beneath my feet.
Your love is a mystery,
How You gently lift me;
When I am surrounded,
Your love carries me.

Hallelujah, hallelujah,
Hallelujah, Your love makes me sing.
Hallelujah, hallelujah,
Hallelujah, Your love makes me sing.

Your love is surprising,
I can feel it rising,
All the joy that's growing
Deep inside of me.
Every time I see You,
All Your goodness shines through,
And I can feel this God song,
Rising up in me.

Your love is better than wine,
Your name like sweetest perfume;
Oh, that You would kiss me
With the kisses of Your mouth
And draw me, draw me after You.
I hear You whisper my name,
And like a moth to the flame
I fly into the fire of Your intimate love
As You draw me, draw me after You.

Draw me after You, (x3)
And let us run together.
(Repeat)

Jesus You're the One, (x3)
That I will love forever.
Jesus You're the One, (x3)
That I will love forever more.

So amazing, so divine,
I am Yours and You are mine.
For such love there are no words,
'Cause loving You is heaven on earth,
'Cause loving You is heaven on earth.

Your whisper to my soul
When I was like a child,
Lifted off the yoke,
Planted fields of hope
In this heart of mine.
You took me as I am,
You knew what I had done,
Still You took my shame,
And You called my name,
I was overcome.

When You broke the bonds
Of how I used to be,
You rolled away the stone,
You set the captive free.

I wanna thank You,
You're the God of mercy;
I wanna thank You, Lord,
For giving me peace.
I wanna thank You,
You're the God who loved me;
I wanna thank You,
You're the God who rescued me.

Brian Houston
Copyright © 2000 Kingsway's Thankyou Music, P.O. Box 75,
Eastbourne, East Sussex, BN23 6NW, UK. tym@kingsway.co.uk.

CCL licence no. _____

You covered all my sin,
Restored to me my youth again,
And I am satisfied.
For You have healed me
And redeemed me,
Crowned my head with endless beauty,
Endless beauty.

I wanna thank You,
You're the God of mercy;
I wanna thank You Lord,
For giving me peace.
I wanna thank You,
You're the God who loved me;
I wanna thank You,
You're the God who rescued me.

You set me apart,
Gave me a new heart,
Filled with compassion
To share Your great love.
Show me Your ways,
I want to know You.
Guide me in truth,
My hope is in You.

That I may dwell in Your house forever,
Lifting up Your name;
Dwell in Your house forever more.
(Repeat)

I'll hold on to You,
My Strength and my Refuge.
Whom shall I fear?
I know You are near.
All of my days I live for You, Lord.
Establish my path,
There's one thing I ask.

Holy Spirit, have Your way.
Sweet anointing teach our hearts,
Our lives, we pray.

Paul Ewing
Copyright © 2000 Paul Ewing/Hillsong Publishing/Kingsway's Thankyou Music,
P.O. Box 75, Eastbourne, East Sussex, BN23 6NW, UK. tym@kingsway.co.uk.
For UK & Europe.

CCL licence no. _____

You shaped the heavens and the earth,
Revealed Your splendour.
You spoke Your life into our hearts,
So we belong to You.

You are the Maker of all things,
First and the Last,
Creation sings praise to You God.
You're reigning in glory,
Ancient of Days,
Your people sing praise to You God.

Creator God, in You all things
Now hold together,
Working Your wonders day by day,
You'll reign forever.

Earth joins with heaven
Declaring Your glory;
Proclaiming the works of Your hands.
(Repeat)

Tim Hughes
Copyright © 2001 Kingsway's Thankyou Music, P.O. Box 75,
Eastbourne, East Sussex, BN23 6NW, UK. tym@kingsway.co.uk.

CCL licence no. _____

You take me by the hand,
And though there are times I don't
        understand,
Your love will never fail
And my heart belongs to You.
Even when the rain clouds break,
And the cold wind blows all around me,
I will not be put to shame.
Lord, my hope is in Your name.
You will carry me on Your shoulders
And lead me home.

Carry me over troubled waters,
Carry me over stormy seas.
When the skies are dark and heavy,
By Your grace You'll carry me.
Though the way can seem uncertain
Because the time of change has come,
You will carry me on Your shoulders
And lead me home.